Richard Lederer and Michael Gilleland

·Literary Trivia·

Richard Lederer has published more than a thousand articles and books about language, including his bestselling *Anguished English, Crazy English, The Miracle of Language,* and *Adventures of a Verbivore.* He was elected International Punster of the year for 1989–90 and has been profiled in magazines as diverse as *The New Yorker, People,* and *The National Enquirer.* Dr. Lederer's weekly column, "Looking for Language," appears in newspapers and magazines throughout the United States. He is the Grammar Grappler for *Writer's Digest,* associate editor of *The Farmers' Almanac,* and a language commentator on National Public Radio.

Michael Gilleland holds degrees from the University of Maine, the University of Virginia, and Central Michigan University. A computer programmer by day, he is an avid reader in his spare time. He lives in Saint Paul, Minnesota, not far from where F. Scott Fitzgerald grew up. This is his first book.

Literary Trivia

Illustrations by Barry Blitt

Literary Trivia

Fun and Games for Book Lovers

RICHARD LEDERER

AND

MICHAEL GILLELAND

VINTAGE BOOKS
A DIVISION OF RANDOM HOUSE, INC.
NEW YORK

A VINTAGE ORIGINAL, DECEMBER 1994
FIRST EDITION

Copyright © 1994 by Richard Lederer and Michael Gilleland

Illustrations copyright © 1994 by Barry Blitt

All rights reserved under International and Pan-American Copyright Conventions.
Published in the United States by Vintage Books, a division of
Random House, Inc., New York, and simultaneously in Canada by
Random House of Canada Limited, Toronto.

Page 235 constitutes an extension of this copyright page.

Library of Congress Cataloging-in-Publication Data
Lederer, Richard, 1938–
Literary trivia : fun and games for book lovers / by Richard
Lederer and Michael Gilleland.—1st ed.
p. cm.
"A Vintage original."
Includes index.
ISBN 0-679-75380-X
1. Authorship—Humor.   2. Literature—Humor.   3. Books and
reading—Humor.   4. Literature—Miscellenea.   5. Books and
reading—Miscellenea.   I. Gilleland, Michael.   II. Title.
PN169.L35   1994
800—dc20   94-8455
CIP

Book Design by Debbie Glasserman

Manufactured in the United States of America
10 9 8 7 6 5 4 3 2

ACKNOWLEDGMENTS

■

Items in "Author! Author! Author!," "Pen-Ultimate Names," "Language Throws the Book at Us," "There's a God in Your Sentence," "Not a Passing Phrase," and "A Man of Many Titles" have appeared in Richard Lederer's *The Play of Words, Crazy English,* and *The Miracle of Language,* all published by Pocket Books.

Special thanks to humorist Louis Phillips for the premise of "Title Match" and many of the examples; to Al Greengold, Sherlockian extraordinaire, for his invaluable contributions to the Doyle section of our Introduction; to Robin Collins, Elisabeth Gilleland, James Kline, William Parrish, and James Pauley for their help and encouragement; and to our editor, Jenna Laslocky, whose work on this book was truly a labor of literary love.

CONTENTS

∎

WORKS

THE BIBLE

MYTHOLOGY

SHAKESPEARE

INTRODUCTION

∎

Thanks to the game Trivial Pursuit and a stack of other general-knowledge quizzes, Americans have been learning all sorts of arcane and exotic facts, from *aardvark,* the first noun in most English dictionaries, to *zyzyva,* a tropical American weevil. What we offer here is a far from trivial book of literary quizzes—from *A,* the scarlet letter worn by Nathaniel Hawthorne's Hester Prynne, to Paul Zindel, who gave us *The Effect of Gamma Rays on Man-in-the-Moon Marigolds.*

Literature lives. Literature endures. Literature prevails. We know this because we know that readers bestow a special kind of life upon people who have existed only in books. Figments though they may be, literary characters can assume a vitality and longevity that pulse more powerfully than flesh and blood.

After many years, the publishers of the children's classic *Charlotte's Web* persuaded E. B. White to record his book on tape. So caught had the author become in the web of his arachnid heroine's life that it took nineteen tapings before White could read aloud the passage about Charlotte's death without his voice cracking.

A century earlier, another writer had been deeply affected by the fate of his heroine. Like most of Charles Dickens's works, *The Old Curiosity Shop* (1841) was published in serial form. The novel won a vast readership on both sides of the Atlantic, and as interest in the fate of the heroine, Little Nell, grew intense, circulation reached the staggering figure of 100,000, a record unequaled by any other of Dickens's major novels. In New York, 6,000 people crowded the wharf where the ship carrying the final *Master Humphrey's Clock* magazine installment was due to dock. As it approached, the crowd's impatience grew to such a pitch that they cried out as one to the sailors, "Does Little Nell die?"

Alas, Little Nell did die, and tens of thousands of readers' hearts broke. The often ferocious literary critic Lord Jeffrey was found weeping with his head on his library table. "You'll be sorry to hear," he sobbed to a friend, "that little Nelly, Boz's little Nelly, is dead." Daniel O'Connell, an Irish M.P., burst out crying, "He should not have killed her," and then, in anguish, threw the book out of the window of the train in which he was traveling. A diary of the time records another reader lamenting, "The villain! The rascal! The bloodthirsty scoundrel! He killed my little Nell! He killed my sweet little child!"

That "bloodthirsty scoundrel" was himself shattered by the loss of his heroine. In a letter to a friend Dickens wrote, "I am the wretchedest of the wretched. It [Nell's death] casts the most horrible shadow upon me, and it is as much as I can do to keep moving at all. . . . Nobody will miss her like I shall."

Even more famous than Charlotte and Little Nell is Arthur Conan Doyle's Sherlock Holmes, the world's first consulting detective. The intrepid sleuth's deerstalker hat, Inverness cape, calabash pipe, and magnifying glass are recognized by readers everywhere, and the stories have been translated into more than sixty languages, from Arabic to Yiddish.

Like the heroes of so many popular stories and myths, Sherlock Holmes was born in poverty and nearly died at birth from neglect. Dr. Arthur Conan Doyle was a novice medical practitioner with a dearth of patients. To while away his time and to help pay a few bills, Doyle took pen in hand and created one of the first detectives to base his work squarely on scientific methods.

The publishing world of 1886 did not grasp the revolutionary implications of Doyle's ideas. Editor after editor returned the manuscript with coldly polite rejection notices. After a year and a half, the young author was about to give up hope, when a publisher finally took a chance and bought the rights for five pounds sterling. In December of 1887, Sherlock Holmes came into the world as an unheralded and unnoticed Yuletide child in *Beeton's Christmas Annual*. When, not long after, *The Strand Magazine* began the monthly serialization of the first dozen short stories entitled "The Adventures of Sherlock Holmes," the issues sold tens of thousands and the public furiously clamored for more.

At the height of success, however, the creator wearied of his creation. He yearned for "higher writing" and felt his special calling to be the historical novel. In December 1893, Doyle introduced into the last story in the Memoirs series the arch-criminal Professor James Moriarty. In "The Final Problem," Holmes and the evil professor wrestle at a cliff's edge in Switzerland. Grasping each other frantically, sleuth and villain plummet to their watery deaths at the foot of the Reichenbach Falls.

With Holmes forever destroyed, Doyle felt he could abandon his mystery stories and turn his authorial eyes to the romantic landscapes of the Middle Ages. He longed to chronicle the clangor of medieval battles, the derring-do of brave knights, and the sighs of lovesick maidens. But the writer's tour back in time would not be that easily booked: Sherlock Holmes had taken on a life of his own, something larger than the will of his creator. The normally staid, stiff-upper-lipped British public was first bereaved, then outraged. Conservative London stockbrokers went to work wearing black armbands in mourning for the loss of their heroic detective. Citizens poured out torrents of letters to editors complaining of Holmes's fate. One woman picketed Doyle's home with a sign branding him a murderer.

The appeals of *The Strand*'s publishers to Doyle's sensibilities and purse went unheeded. For the next eight years Holmes lay dead at the bottom of the Swiss falls while Doyle branched out into historical fiction, science fiction, horror stories, and medical stories.

Finally, Doyle could resist the pressures from publisher and public no more. He wrote what may be the best of all the Holmes stories, "The Hound of the Baskervilles," which was immediately serialized in *The Strand*. As the story made clear, Holmes had not returned from his demise as reported in 1893. This tale was merely a reminiscence, set in 1888. Still, the reappearance of Sherlock Holmes fired the public imagination— and its enthusiasm: readers again queued up by the thousands to buy the monthly installments of the magazine. In 1903, ten years after his "death," Doyle's detective rose up from his watery grave in the Reichenbach Falls, his logical wonders to perform for the whole world.

"The Return of Sherlock Holmes," the series of thirteen stories that brought back Doyle's hero, was greeted eagerly by patient British readers whose appetites had been whetted by "Hound," and the author continued writing stories of his detective right into 1927. When in 1930 Arthur Conan Doyle died at age seventy-one, readers around the world mourned his passing. Newspaper cartoons portraying a grieving Sherlock Holmes captured the public's sense of irreparable loss.

Such is the power of mythic literature that the creation has outlived his creator. Letters and packages from all over the world still come addressed to "Sherlock Holmes" at 221-B Baker Street, where they are answered by a full-time secretary. Only Santa Claus gets more mail, at least just before Christmastime. More movies have been made about Holmes than about Dracula, Frankenstein, Robin Hood, and Rocky, combined. Sherlock Holmes stories written by post-Doylean authors vastly outnumber the sixty that Doyle produced. More than one hundred and fifty societies in homage to Sherlock Holmes are active in the United States alone.

However many times the progenitor tried to finish off his hero, by murder or retirement or flat refusal to write any more adventures, the Great Detective lives, vigilant and deductive as ever, protecting the humble from the evils that lurk in the very heart of our so-called civilization. Despite his "death" a hundred years ago, Sherlock Holmes has never died. Readers around the world simply won't let him.

If you have read this far into this Introduction, you are almost certainly a person for whom the people who live in books are very much alive. We have constructed the posers in these pages from material that we believe is in the conscious or unconscious repertoire of people like you who love to read. As with any true challenge, however, some of the questions can be answered easily, while others will cause head-scratching among even the most bookish.

We wrote *Literary Trivia* to show just how much fun the study of great—and sometimes more-popular-than-great—literature can be. The Roman poet Lucretius explained his method of teaching in his didactic poem "The Nature of Things." He said that he treated the passing along of abstruse subject matter in the same way that a physician, intending to administer medicine, might coat the rim of the cup with honey. Play is the honey of this book. Above all else, we intend to amuse and entertain you with games and quizzes that test your literary literacy. We also expect that you will learn or be reminded of some of the greatest literature in the English language, along with a selection of foreign classics. Ultimately, you may be inspired to read or reread some of the masterpieces mentioned along the way. If you are, run—don't walk—to your nearest library or bookstore.

We urge you to take control of this book, to do it "your way." Feel free to use the lengthy index of authors and titles as an initial review. We have saved "The Bible," "Mythology," and "Shakespeare" for the second half of our book; you may decide to begin with these three pillars of literature and work through the first half second. In many games we ask you to match titles, characters, works, and authors in some way. You can make these challenges more difficult by covering up the right-hand column and looking at just the entries in the left-hand column. Most readers will play the games as a species of solitaire; we invite you to grapple with the quizzes with other book lovers, if that will add to your social and intellectual pleasure. You, dear reader, are the one in charge.

Benjamin Franklin was a guest at a Paris dinner party when a question was posed: What condition of man most deserves pity? Each guest proposed an example of a miserable situation. When Franklin's turn came, he responded, "A lonesome man on a rainy day who does not know how to read." Because you are still holding this volume in your hand, you must be a bibliophile. As a member of that happy and privileged band, you will never be lonely. Forevermore you have the company and conversation of thousands of men and women, ancient and contemporary, learned and light, who have set their humanity to paper and cobbled language into literature.

—Richard Lederer
Michael Gilleland

Authors -

Hardy

Chaucer

Austen

Faulkner

Twain

AUTHORIAL ANECDOTES

■

Henry David Thoreau, who wrote *Walden,* helped runaway slaves escape to Canada and became one of the first Americans to speak in defense of John Brown. When Thoreau spent a day in jail for acting on the dictates of his conscience, he was visited by friend Ralph Waldo Emerson.

Emerson asked, "Henry, why are you here?"

Thoreau answered, "Waldo, why are you *not* here?"

Within the brief compass of a biographical incident we can sometimes catch and crystallize the essence of a person's character. Here are our favorite anecdotes about authors, each of whom you are asked to identify:

1. When he was ninety years of age, this Greek tragedian was brought before a court of law by his sons, who sought to have him declared senile and thus incompetent to manage his estate. In his own defense, the playwright read aloud passages from his *Oedipus at Colonus,* which he had recently completed but not yet staged. The jury confirmed his competency, chastised his sons, and escorted him home as an honor.

2. President Abraham Lincoln took this abolitionist author of *Uncle Tom's Cabin* by the hand and asked, "So this is the little lady who made this big war."

3. This British writer's rags-to-riches life was more remarkable than any of his sentimental stories. Born into an impoverished family and having worked as a child slave in a London blacking factory, he became, at the age of twenty-five, the most popular author in England.

4. This reclusive American writer was depicted in W. P. Kinsella's novel *Shoeless Joe*. When the subject threatened to sue, he was replaced in the film version, titled *Field of Dreams,* by a fictitious writer named Terrence Mann, who was portrayed by James Earl Jones.

5. This writer, critic, and humorist once arrived simultaneously at a narrow doorway with the playwright, journalist, and politician Clare Boothe Luce.

"Age before beauty," said Mrs. Luce, stepping aside.

"Pearls before swine," purred our writer as she glided through the doorway.

6. Born a slave in Maryland and escaping in 1838, this powerful orator became the leading African American in the abolitionist movement. He recruited black soldiers to fight in the Civil War and ultimately produced three autobiographies.

7. At the height of this British writer's popularity, he is said to have earned about a dollar a word. This inspired a certain autograph hound, who had been unsuccessful in obtaining the great man's signature, to try again. He sent off a letter that he was sure would produce the desired result: "I see you get $1 a word for your writing. I enclose a check for $1. Please send me a sample." The writer replied by postcard—unsigned: "Thanks."

8. In less than nine years, this London man of letters almost single-handedly produced the first authoritative dictionary of the English language, a feat that took academy committees in France and Italy decades to accomplish.

9. This politically active English poet became completely blind at the age of forty-five and afterward wrote a sonnet, "On His Blindness," and the epic poem *Paradise Lost*.

10. This English Lake Poet fell asleep, perhaps under the

influence of opium, and dreamed a complete vision of a poem, "Kubla Khan." When he awoke, he immediately set to writing out his vision but was interrupted by "a person on business from Porlock."

11. The poet Lord Byron challenged a group of his friends to create their own ghost stories. From that challenge came the tale *Frankenstein,* written by this twenty-one-year-old wife of another romantic poet.

12. When the first edition of this American poet's collection of poems appeared in 1855, the *Boston Intelligencer* said in its review: "The author should be kicked out from all decent society as below the level of the brute. He must be some escaped lunatic raving in pitiable delirium." The collection went through nine more editions and gained a large, enthusiastic readership in the United States and England.

13. Only seven of this New England woman's poems were published during her lifetime, and she left instructions that all of her manuscripts be destroyed. Today she and her contemporary in the question above are the two most widely read and influential American poets of the nineteenth century.

14. This New England writer had 706 of one of his unsold books returned to him by a book dealer. In a journal entry he wrote, "I now have a library of nearly 900 volumes, over 700 of which I wrote myself."

15. This American humorist and member of the famed Algonquin Round Table once quipped, "It took me fifteen years to discover that I had no talent for writing, but I couldn't give it up because by that time I was too famous."

16. Worn down by poverty, this unknown Scottish poet resolved to emigrate to Jamaica in 1786. To finance the journey, he gathered together some of his poems in a thin volume. The small collection took Scotland by storm, and the young man went on to become his country's national poet.

17. This London pre-Romantic poet was also a painter, engraver, and spiritual visionary. He was struck with what is

known as eidectic sight, a quality that allowed him to see visions as well as imagine them. When he was but a child, he claimed to have seen the prophet Ezekiel in a tree. Years later, his wife and he sat nude in their garden reciting passages from *Paradise Lost* as if they were in the Garden of Eden. His vivid engravings designed to accompany his poems made him the world's first multimedia artist.

18. As a young cadet, this American writer was expelled from West Point for reporting to a march wearing nothing but white gloves.

19. This British essayist and several literary friends were asked one evening what book they would prefer to have with them if stranded on a desert isle. "The complete works of Shakespeare," said one writer without hesitation. "I'd choose the Bible," asserted another. "I would choose," replied our writer, *"Thomas's Guide to Practical Shipbuilding."*

20. This British writer showed his first novel, *The White Peacock,* to his coal-miner father. After struggling through half a page, the father asked, "And what dun they gie thee for that, lad?"

"Fifty pounds, Father," the son answered.

"Fifty pounds!" exclaimed the dumbfounded father. "Fifty pounds! An' tha's niver done a day's hard work in thy life!"

21. When he was a young busboy in a Washington, D.C., hotel, this American poet left a packet of his poems next to the poet Vachel Lindsay's plate. Lindsay helped to launch the young man's career, and the busboy became the leading figure in the Harlem Renaissance.

22 and 23. When a popular Jazz Age American novelist remarked to another famous writer that "the rich are very different from you and me," the latter replied, "Yes, they have more money." Name the two authors.

24. When this Russian writer's first novel was well received in 1846, he joined a revolutionary group that was infiltrated by the authorities. Together with several associates, he was tried

and sentenced to be shot. The execution was a cruel hoax, and, at the very last minute, the sentence was commuted to years of hard labor in Siberia. Ten years later he returned to St. Petersburg as a conservative and became one of the very greatest of all Russian authors.

25. When this Irish playwright was stopped by U.S. customs in New York, he proclaimed, "I have nothing to declare except my genius."

26. A nineteen-month-old girl lay dying in a London hospital. Her condition baffled the doctors until a nurse noted that the patient's symptoms were remarkably like those of an infant in the detective novel *Pale Horse*. The nurse's suggestion that the patient could have thallium poisoning was confirmed by tests. Given proper treatment, the baby recovered. Who was the famous author of *Pale Horse*?

27. This conjurer of animal fables is said to have been a deformed black slave who lived in the sixth century B.C. According to tradition, he used his fables to bolster his arguments and, ultimately, to win his freedom.

28. The science-fiction stories of this French author were called "dreams come true." So prophetic was his description of a periscope in *Twenty Thousand Leagues under the Sea* that a few years later the actual inventor of the instrument was refused permission for an original patent.

29. After reaching forty, this housewife and mother of five began writing her first books—the Earth's Children fictional saga. The series has gone on to become one of the fastest-selling in publishing history.

30. This American poet was asked to compose a poem and read it at John F. Kennedy's inauguration in 1961. When the sun's glare prevented him from reading the poem at the occasion, he instead recited "The Gift Outright" from memory.

ANSWERS

1. Sophocles 2. Harriet Beecher Stowe 3. Charles Dickens 4. J. D. Salinger 5. Dorothy Parker 6. Frederick Douglass 7. Rudyard Kipling 8. Samuel Johnson 9. John Milton 10. Samuel Taylor Coleridge

11. Mary Wollstonecraft Shelley 12. Walt Whitman 13. Emily Dickinson 14. Henry David Thoreau 15. Robert Benchley 16. Robert Burns 17. William Blake 18. Edgar Allan Poe 19. G. K. Chesterton 20. D. H. Lawrence

21. Langston Hughes 22 and 23. F. Scott Fitzgerald and Ernest Hemingway 24. Fyodor Dostoevsky 25. Oscar Wilde 26. Agatha Christie 27. Aesop 28. Jules Verne 29. Jean Auel 30. Robert Frost

MOONLIGHTING FOR SIXPENCE

■

If Dr. Johnson was correct when he thundered that "no man but a blockhead ever wrote except for money," most writers are blockheads. They write for the love, not the money.

"In America you can make a fortune as a writer, but not a living," wrote James Michener, who certainly knows a lot about making a fortune as a blockbuster novelist. In a 1978 survey of hundreds of members of P.E.N., the international writers' organization, the median annual income from writing was $4,700, with 68 percent making under $10,000 and 9 percent earning nothing.

Worth a fortune today, the twenty-two plates that William Blake engraved from 1823 to 1825 illustrating the Book of Job earned him barely two or three pounds a week.

Even William Shakespeare, the greatest of them all, was paid no more than eight pounds apiece for his plays, never more than twenty pounds a year. He was thus obliged to become part of the quiz below.

American writers have fared no better: "To coin one's brain into silver," Edgar Allan Poe once wrote, "is to my thinking the hardest job in the world." It took him a year and a half to pry his ten-dollar payment loose from the *New York Mirror* for a

poem the paper had printed. That poem was "The Raven."
Ralph Waldo Emerson customarily received five dollars for each
lecture he delivered and often had to argue with his sponsors
about whether or not the oats for his horse were included in the
payment.

The preternaturally prolific Henry James wrote sardonically
to Edith Wharton, "With the proceeds of my last novel, I
purchased a small go-cart, or hand-barrow, on which my guests'
luggage is wheeled from the station to my house. It needs a coat
of paint. With the proceeds of my next novel I shall have it
painted."

Because most writers cannot survive by their pens, they must
often work in other professions, not always to their liking. While
writing *Barchester Towers, The Eustace Diamonds,* and almost fifty
other novels, Anthony Trollope was a British postal official.
Each day he arose at 5:30 A.M. and wrote a thousand words an
hour for two and a half hours before going to work. During his
thirty-three years of service, he invented the street-corner mail-
box, making him doubly a man of letters.

Eudora Welty wrote about the career of another postal employee, this one a postmaster in Oxford, Mississippi: "Let us
imagine that here and now, we're all in the old university post
office and living in the '20s. We've come up to the stamp
window to buy a 2-cent stamp, but we see nobody there. We
knock and then we pound, and then we pound again and there's
not a sound back there. So we holler his name, and at last here
he is, William Faulkner. We interrupted him. . . . When he
should have been putting up the mail and selling stamps at the
window up front, he was out of sight in the back writing lyric
poems."

When Henry Miller quit his job as a branch manager for
Western Union, he vowed never to work for anyone else again.
Of his four and a half years of employment he said, "It was a
period comparable, for me, to Dostoevsky's stay in Siberia."

The authors listed below earned their daily bread by means

other than their pens. Match each writer with the profession he
or she followed:

Matthew Arnold	accountant
Honoré de Balzac	ad writer
Ambrose Bierce	apothecary–surgeon
John Bunyan	architect
Lewis Carroll	attorney
Daniel Defoe	Civil War general
Charles Dickens	customs house surveyor
John Donne	dentist
Arthur Conan Doyle	diplomat
Paul Laurence Dunbar	doctor
Zane Grey	elevator operator
Thomas Hardy	embezzler
Nathaniel Hawthorne	entomologist
James Herriot	gold seeker
Eric Hoffer	imperial policeman
Oliver Wendell Holmes	inspector of schools
Gerard Manley Hopkins	insurance attorney
A. E. Housman	Jesuit priest
Langston Hughes	law clerk
Washington Irving	lens grinder
Samuel Johnson	librarian
John Keats	longshoreman
Rudyard Kipling	mathematician
Charles Lamb	member of acting company
Jack London	Napoleonic dragoon
Herman Melville	newspaper columnist
John Milton	newspaper editor
Marianne Moore	newspaper reporter
Vladimir Nabokov	ophthalmologist
O. Henry	patent office clerk
George Orwell	pediatrician
Samuel Richardson	pencil maker

Antoine de Saint-Exupéry	pilot
Dorothy Sayers	political pamphleteer
Sir Walter Scott	preacher
William Shakespeare	printer
Benedict de Spinoza	professor of Anglo-Saxon
Stendhal	schoolmaster
Wallace Stevens	seaman
Henry David Thoreau	steamboat pilot
J.R.R. Tolkien	tinker
Mark Twain	tobacco merchant
Lew Wallace	veterinarian
William Carlos Williams	waiter

ANSWERS

Matthew Arnold—inspector of schools; Honoré de Balzac—law clerk; Ambrose Bierce—newspaper columnist; John Bunyan—tinker; Lewis Carroll—mathematician

Daniel Defoe—tobacco merchant; Charles Dickens—newspaper reporter; John Donne—preacher; Arthur Conan Doyle—ophthalmologist, physician; Paul Laurence Dunbar—elevator operator

Zane Grey—dentist; Thomas Hardy—architect; Nathaniel Hawthorne—customs house surveyor, diplomat; James Herriot—veterinarian; Eric Hoffer—longshoreman

Oliver Wendell Holmes—physician; Gerard Manley Hopkins—Jesuit priest, preacher; A. E. Housman—patent office clerk; Langston Hughes—waiter; Washington Irving—diplomat

Samuel Johnson—schoolmaster; John Keats—apothecary-surgeon; Rudyard Kipling—newspaper editor; Charles Lamb—accountant; Jack London—gold seeker

Herman Melville—seaman; John Milton—political pamphleteer; Marianne Moore—librarian; Vladimir Nabokov—entomologist; O. Henry—embezzler

George Orwell—imperial policeman, political pamphleteer; Samuel Richardson—printer; Antoine de Saint-Exupéry—pilot; Dorothy Sayers—ad writer; Sir Walter Scott—attorney

William Shakespeare—member of acting company; Benedict de Spinoza—lens grinder; Stendhal—Napoleonic dragoon; Wallace Stevens—insurance attorney; Henry David Thoreau—pencil maker, schoolmaster

J.R.R. Tolkien—professor of Anglo-Saxon; Mark Twain—steamboat pilot, newspaper reporter; Lew Wallace—Civil War general; William Carlos Williams—pediatrician

AUTHOR! AUTHOR! AUTHOR!

∎

On a February day in 1892 Charles Buzzell, who had lain unconscious for nine days without food and water, was virtually DOA by the time he got to St. Vincent's Hospital. Doctors in the emergency room battled the odds to keep him alive—and won. The heroism of the medical staff so impressed Buzzell's married sister that when she gave birth to a daughter not long thereafter, she honored the institution by making it part of the baby's name. That's how poet Edna St. Vincent Millay came to be named—in dactylic trimeter!—for a New York hospital.

Edna St. Vincent Millay is a trinomial, that is, a person who is best known by three names. How many trinomials do you hear or read about in today's news? Sure, a handful of triple names comes to mind—Andrew Lloyd Webber, Jack Kent Cooke, Sandra Day O'Connor, Helen Gurley Brown, Norman Vincent Peale, John Kenneth Galbraith, Alan Jay Lerner, Margaret Chase Smith, Joyce Carol Oates, Catherine Drinker Bowen, Mary Higgins Clark, and John Gregory Dunne. But this small band of exceptions serves only to remind us of an age gone by when to be known by three names was nothing out of the ordinary.

To gain a glimpse into an age when trinomials were more in
fashion, look at the middle names of dead poets and other writers
who were best known by three names:

1._____Allan_____		32._____Jean_____
2._____Ames_____		33._____Kinnan_____
3._____Anne_____		34._____Laurence_____
4._____Arlington_____		35._____Lawrence_____
5._____Babington_____		36._____Lee_____
6._____Bailey____		37._____Louis_____
7._____Barrett_____		38._____Madox_____
8._____Bashevis_____		39._____Makepeace_____
9._____Beecher_____		40._____Manley_____
10._____Bernard_____		41._____Maria_____
11._____Boothe_____		42._____May_____
12._____Branch_____		43._____Millington_____
13._____Brinsley_____		44._____Neale_____
14._____Butler_____		45._____Orne_____
15._____Bysshe_____		46._____Payson_____
16._____Carlos_____		47._____Penn_____
17._____Chandler_____		48._____Peter_____
18._____Christian_____		49._____Rice_____
19._____Clarke_____		50._____Russell_____
20._____Clerihew_____		51._____Savage_____
21._____Conan_____		52._____Stanley_____
22._____Crowe_____		53._____Taylor_____
23._____Cullen_____		54._____Vincent_____
24._____David_____		55._____Wadsworth_____
25._____Dean_____		56._____Waldo_____
26._____Everett_____		57._____Ward_____
27._____Fenimore_____		58._____Weldon_____
28._____Gabriel_____		59._____Wendell_____
29._____Gould_____		60._____Whitcomb_____
30._____Greenleaf_____		61._____Wing_____
31._____Ingalls_____		62._____Wollstonecraft_____

Other writers prefer to be known by their initials rather than their full names. Take the initiative and match the writerly initials in the left-hand column with the last names in the right-hand column:

63. A. A.	Andrews
64. A. B.	Auden
65. A. E.	Ballard
66. A. J.	Cronin
67. B. F.	cummings
68. C. P.	Doctorow
69. C. S.	Donleavy
70. D. H.	Du Bois
71. D. M.	Eliot
72. E. B.	Forster
73. e. e.	Frank Baum
74. E. L.	Guthrie
75. E. M.	Henry
76. F.	Hinton
77. H.	Housman
78. H. G.	James
79. H. H.	Lawrence
80. H. L.	Lewis
81. H. P.	Lovecraft
82. J. B.	Mencken
83. J. D.	Merwin
84. J. G.	Milne
85. J. P.	Munro
86. J.R.R.	Perelman
87. L.	Priestley
88. O.	Pritchett
89. P.D.	Rider Haggard
90. P. G.	Salinger
91. P. L.	Scott Fitzgerald
92. S. E.	Skinner

93.	S. J.	Snow
94.	T. S.	Somerset Maugham
95.	V. C.	Thomas
96.	V. S.	Tolkien
97.	W.	Travers
98.	W.E.B.	Wells
99.	W. H.	White
100.	W. S.	Wodehouse

ANSWERS

1. Edgar Poe 2. Ben Williams 3. Katherine Porter 4. Edwin Robinson 5. Thomas Macaulay 6. Thomas Aldrich 7. Elizabeth Browning 8. Isaac Singer 9. Harriet Stowe 10. George Shaw 11. Clare Luce 12. James Cabell 13. Richard Sheridan 14. William Yeats 15. Percy Shelley 16. William Williams 17. Joel Harris 18. Hans Andersen 19. Clement Moore 20. Edmund Bentley

21. Arthur Doyle 22. John Ransom 23. William Bryant 24. Henry Thoreau 25. William Howells 26. Edward Hale 27. James Cooper 28. Dante Rossetti 29. James Cozzens 30. John Whittier

31. Laura Wilder 32. George Nathan 33. Marjorie Rawlings 34. Paul Dunbar 35. Ernest Thayer 36. Edgar Masters 37. Robert Stevenson 38. Ford Ford 39. William Thackeray 40. Gerard Hopkins

41. Erich Remarque 42. Louisa Alcott 43. John Synge 44. Zora Hurston 45. Sarah Jewett 46. Albert Terhune 47. Robert Warren 48. Finley Dunne 49. Edgar Burroughs 50. James Lowell

51. William Landor 52. Erle Gardner 53. Samuel Coleridge 54. Stephen Benet 55. Henry Longfellow 56. Ralph Emerson 57. Julia Howe or Henry Beecher 58. James Johnson 59. Oliver Holmes 60. James Riley

61. Arthur Pinero 62. Mary Shelley 63. Milne 64. Guthrie 65. Housman 66. Cronin 67. Skinner 68. Snow 69. Lewis 70. Lawrence

71. Thomas 72. White 73. cummings 74. Doctorow 75. Forster 76. Scott Fitzgerald 77. Rider Haggard 78. Wells 79. Munro 80. Mencken

81. Lovecraft 82. Priestley 83. Salinger 84. Ballard 85. Donleavy 86. Tolkien 87. Frank Baum 88. Henry 89. James 90. Wodehouse

91. Travers 92. Hinton 93. Perelman 94. Eliot 95. Andrews 96. Pritchett 97. Somerset Maugham 98. Du Bois 99. Auden 100. Merwin

PEN–ULTIMATE NAMES

■

The authors of *Alice's Adventures in Wonderland, Silas Marner,* and *Nineteen Eighty-Four* have something in common besides being British. They are all better known by their pseudonyms, or pen names, than by their real names.

It's hard to imagine why a writer who goes to the trouble of scratching out a work of art would want to be known by another identity. On the other hand, if you were born Amandine Lucie Aurore Dupin, Jacques Anatole François Thibault, or Aleksey Maximovich Peshkov, you might adopt the nom de plume of George Sand, Anatole France, or Maxim Gorky. And, if it's efficiency you seek, it's obvious that Molière, Voltaire, and Stendhal are considerably more compact than Jean-Baptiste Poquelin, François-Marie Arouet, and Marie-Henri Beyle.

Here are brief biographies of fifteen famous writers who made the change. From the information supplied, identify each nom de plume:

1. Eric Arthur Blair wrote a long fable about a society in which some animals are more equal than others. In 1948 he published a novel about a nightmarish society of the future, one in which everybody had a Big Brother.

2. Samuel Langhorne Clemens was a steamboat pilot before he became a writer. In 1863 he took on the pen name that was a nostalgic reminder of his riverboat days.

3. In March 1836, what has been described as the most successful writing career in history was launched with the publication of *The Posthumous Papers of the Pickwick Club*. The author, of course, was Charles Dickens. In 1833, when he was only twenty-one, Dickens began contributing stories and essays to magazines and published them pseudonymously in a collection called *Sketches by_____*.

4. Charles Lutwidge Dodgson was fascinated with words, logic, and little girls. Out of these interests he fashioned a wonderland of characters—Humpty Dumptys, Jabberwocks, Mad Hatters, and White Rabbits.

5. Famous for her novels describing life in nineteenth-century England, including *Adam Bede, Silas Marner,* and *Middlemarch,* Mary Ann Evans adopted a masculine pen name, by George.

6. He meant what he said, and he said what he meant, and his books have pleased children one hundred percent. Theodor Giesel conjured up and drew creatures that now exist in the imaginations of generations of children.

7. Convicted for embezzlement, William Sydney Porter spent almost four years in prison, where he began his career as an immensely popular writer of short stories. Most of his tales are about life in New York and are marked by surprise endings.

8. Late in life, after a long career as a veterinary surgeon, James Alfred Wight began writing books that communicated his profound affection for animals. The titles of two of those books are taken from a hymn that begins, "All things bright and beautiful, all creatures great and small."

9. Józef Korzeniowski was born in Poland and grew up speaking no English until he was seventeen, yet he became one of the greatest stylists ever to use the English language. A sailor as a youth, Korzeniowski is most famous for his stories and novels of the sea.

10. Hector Hugh Munro was killed in action during World War I. He left behind him the charming, often biting short stories to which he signed a pseudonym borrowed from *The Rubáiyát*.

11. An unpublished Atlanta writer named Peggy Marsh submitted an incomplete manuscript that filled a large suitcase. The title of the novel was to be "Tomorrow Is Another Day," and its heroine was to be called Pansy. After a great number of changes, including the title and name of the heroine, the book was published in 1936 and quickly became an all-time best-seller, inspiring a blockbuster movie and, fifty years after that, a blockbuster sequel.

12. Russian-born Yiddish author Solomon Rabinowitz took his pen name from a Hebrew expression meaning "peace be unto you."

13. British novelist and critic John B. Wilson is most famous for *A Clockwork Orange*. His works often combine word play and a grim view of life.

14. Baroness Karen Blixen, a Danish author who wrote primarily in English, managed a coffee plantation in British East Africa. She is best known for her tales and her autobiography drawn from her African experience.

15. For many years, Manfred Lee and his cousin Frederic Dannay functioned as one author, an eccentric bookworm who allegedly wrote about his adventures as a detective.

ANSWERS

1. George Orwell 2. Mark Twain 3. Boz 4. Lewis Carroll 5. George Eliot 6. Dr. Seuss 7. O. Henry 8. James Herriot 9. Joseph Conrad 10. Saki

11. Margaret Mitchell 12. Sholem Aleichem 13. Anthony Burgess 14. Isak Dinesen 15. Ellery Queen

ALSO KNOWN AS . . .

■

What do these four sentences have in common?:

WE ALL MAKE HIS PRAISE.
I SWEAR HE'S LIKE A LAMP.
"HAS WILL A PEER?" I ASK ME.
AH, I SPEAK A SWELL RIME.

The answer is that they are all anagrams of the name William Shakespeare; that is, each sentence is a rearrangement of all the letters in the Bard's name to make a meaningful statement.

John Bunyan anagrammed his own name at a time when *i* and *j* were interchangeable:

> *Witness my name, if anagram'd to thee,*
> *The letters make 'Nu hony in a B.'*

One of Jonathan Swift's pseudonyms was Cadenus, an anagram of *Decanus,* Latin for *dean.* Honoré de Balzac used R'Hoone, an anagram of his first name. Molière was satirized in Le Boulanger de Chalussay's play *Élomire the Hypochondriac* (1670). Élomire is an anagram of Molière. Lewis Carroll is a Latinized form in reverse of the first two names of Charles Lutwidge Dodgson.

Unscramble the following authorial anagrams. The rearrangement may be of the first, middle, or last names, or any combination thereof:

1. Won half the New World's glory (American poet)
2. Person whom all read (American thinker, poet, and essayist)
3. He'll do in mellow verse (American poet)
4. Azure pond (American poet)
5. Toilets (American and British poet)
6. Last Scot writer (Scottish novelist and poet)
7. Hail! Nate hath renown (American fiction writer)
8. Alien do feed (English novelist)
9. Dig over Tom's hill (English novelist and playwright)
10. Gave us a damned clever satire (Spanish novelist)
11. Greatest idealist born (Pre-Raphaelite poet)
12. Our best novelist, Señor (English novelist and poet)
13. Vivian Darkbloom (Russian-born novelist)

William Shakespeare's Juliet asks, "What's in a name?" She might have also inquired, "What's in a nickname?" The answer is "plenty." Even the Bard of Avon didn't escape without one. Now match the nicknames with the authors they describe:

14. The Bard of Rydal Mount   Aristotle
15. The Belle of Amherst   Roger Bacon
16. Darwin's Bulldog   Democritus
17. Doctor Mirabilis   Emily Dickinson
18. The Good Gray Poet   Ralph Waldo Emerson
19. The Laughing Philosopher   Philip Freneau
20. The Lexicographer   Ernest Hemingway
21. The Mantuan Swan   Homer
22. Moor   Thomas Henry Huxley
23. Papa   Samuel Johnson
24. The Poet of the American   Karl Marx
    Revolution

25. The Sage of Concord	Pindar
26. The Stargirite	Alexander Pope
27. The Swan of Meander	Sir Walter Scott
28. The Theban Eagle	Vergil
29. The Wasp of Twickenham	Walt Whitman
30. The Wizard of the North	William Wordsworth

ANSWERS

1. Henry Wadsworth Longfellow 2. Ralph Waldo Emerson 3. Oliver Wendell Holmes 4. Ezra Pound 5. T. S. Eliot 6. Sir Walter Scott 7. Nathaniel Hawthorne 8. Daniel Defoe 9. Oliver Goldsmith 10. Miguel de Cervantes Saavedra

11. Dante Gabriel Rossetti 12. Robert Louis Stevenson 13. Vladimir Nabokov 14. William Wordsworth 15. Emily Dickinson 16. Thomas Henry Huxley 17. Roger Bacon 18. Walt Whitman 19. Democritus 20. Samuel Johnson

21. Vergil 22. Karl Marx 23. Ernest Hemingway 24. Philip Freneau 25. Ralph Waldo Emerson 26. Aristotle 27. Homer 28. Pindar 29. Alexander Pope 30. Sir Walter Scott

NOT-SO-PRIVATE LIVES

■

In *The Innocents Abroad,* Mark Twain observed, "At certain periods it becomes the dearest ambition of a man to keep a faithful record of his performances in a book." "On my side," added Henry David Thoreau in the first chapter of *Walden,* "I require of every writer, first or last, a simple and sincere account of his own life." In fact, most authors pour their own experiences into all their works, sometimes to the extent of presenting autobiographies.

Autobiographical titles can be misleading. William Styron's *The Confessions of Nat Turner* purports to be told by the actual slave leader. Neither *The Memoirs of Barry Lyndon, Esq., Written by Himself* nor *The Life and Strange Surprizing Adventures of Robinson Crusoe, of York, Mariner . . . Written by Himself* was written by "themselves"; their authors were William Makepeace Thackeray and Daniel Defoe respectively. *The Autobiography of Malcolm X* was in large part ghostwritten by Alex Haley. *The Autobiography of Miss Jean Pittman* was the product of Ernest Gaines, while *The Autobiography of Alice B. Toklas* was written by her friend Gertrude Stein and deals very little with Ms. Toklas. *Black Beauty: The Autobiography of a Horse* was written not by the beloved hoofer but by Anna Sewell.

Match the fifty authors below with their autobiographical works:

Jane Addams	*Across Spoon River*
Maya Angelou	*An American Childhood*
Isaac Asimov	*Apologia pro Vita Sua*
Saint Augustine	*A Backward Glance*
Russell Baker	*The Bell Jar*
Brendan Behan	*Black Boy*
Claude Brown	*Black Ice*
Pearl Buck	*Blackberry Winter*
John Bunyan	*Borstal Boy*
Lorene Cary	*Confessions*
Eldridge Cleaver	*Confessions of an English Opium Eater*
e. e. cummings	*Dawn*
Richard Henry Dana	*De Profundis*
Dante	*The Diary of a Young Girl*
Clarence Day	*Down These Mean Streets*
Thomas de Quincey	*The Enormous Room*
Annie Dillard	*Grace Abounding to the Chief of Sinners*
Isak Dinesen	*Growing Up*
Frederick Douglass	*Happy Days*
Theodore Dreiser	*I Know Why the Caged Bird Sings*
Anne Frank	*I Wonder As I Wander*
Johann Wolfgang von Goethe	*In Memory Yet Green*
Maxim Gorky	*In My Father's Court*
Graham Greene	*In the World*
Adolf Hitler	*Life Among the Savages*
Frank Harris	*Life With Father*
Langston Hughes	*The Making of an American*
Shirley Jackson	*Manchild in the Promised Land*
Helen Keller	*Mein Kampf*
Robert MacNeil	*Memories of a Catholic Girlhood*
Beryl Markham	*My Life and Freedom*

Edgar Lee Masters	*My Life and Hard Times*
Mary McCarthy	*My Life and Loves*
Margaret Mead	*My Several Worlds*
H. L. Mencken	*The New Life*
John Henry Newman	*Night*
Sylvia Plath	*Out of Africa*
Jacob Riis	*Out of My Life and Thoughts*
Albert Schweitzer	*Poetry and Truth*
Isaac Bashevis Singer	*Portrait of the Artist as a Young Dog*
Dylan Thomas	*Roughing It*
Piri Thomas	*A Sort of Life*
James Thurber	*Soul on Ice*
Mark Twain	*The Story of My Life*
Booker T. Washington	*This Boy's Life*
Edith Wharton	*Twenty Years at Hull House*
Elie Wiesel	*Two Years Before the Mast*
Oscar Wilde	*Up From Slavery*
Tobias Wolff	*West with the Night*
Richard Wright	*Wordstruck*

Answers

Jane Addams, *Twenty Years at Hull House;* Maya Angelou, *I Know Why the Caged Bird Sings;* Isaac Asimov, *In Memory Yet Green;*

Saint Augustine, *Confessions;* Russell Baker, *Growing Up;* Brendan Behan, *Borstal Boy;* Claude Brown, *Manchild in the Promised Land;* Pearl Buck, *My Several Worlds;* John Bunyan, *Grace Abounding to the Chief of Sinners;* Lorene Cary, *Black Ice*

Eldridge Cleaver, *Soul on Ice;* e. e. cummings, *The Enormous Room;* Richard Henry Dana, *Two Years Before the Mast;* Dante, *The New Life;* Clarence Day, *Life With Father;* Thomas de Quincey, *Confessions of an English Opium Eater;* Annie Dillard, *An American Childhood;* Isak Dinesen, *Out of Africa;* Frederick Douglass, *My Life and Freedom;* Theodore Dreiser, *Dawn*

Anne Frank, *The Diary of a Young Girl;* Johann Wolfgang von Goethe, *Poetry and Truth;* Maxim Gorky, *In the World;* Graham Greene, *A Sort of Life;* Frank Harris, *My Life and Loves;* Adolf Hitler, *Mein Kampf* (originally titled *Four and a Half Years of Struggle Against Lies, Stupidity, and Cowardice,* prompting critic Timothy Foote to observe, "Everyone needs an editor"); Langston Hughes, *I Wonder As I Wander;* Shirley Jackson, *Life Among the Savages;* Helen Keller, *The Story of My Life;* Robert MacNeil, *Wordstruck*

Beryl Markham, *West with the Night;* Edgar Lee Masters, *Across Spoon River;* Mary McCarthy, *Memories of a Catholic Girlhood;* Margaret Mead, *Blackberry Winter;* H. L. Mencken, *Happy Days;* John Henry Newman, *Apologia pro Vita Sua;* Sylvia Plath, *The Bell Jar;* Jacob Riis, *The Making of an American;* Albert Schweitzer, *Out of My Life and Thoughts;* Isaac Bashevis Singer, *In My Father's Court*

Dylan Thomas, *Portrait of the Artist as a Young Dog;* Piri Thomas, *Down These Mean Streets;* James Thurber, *My Life and Hard Times;* Mark Twain, *Roughing It;* Booker T. Washington, *Up from Slavery;* Edith Wharton, *A Backward Glance;* Elie Wiesel, *Night;* Oscar Wilde, *De Profundis;* Tobias Wolff, *This Boy's Life;* Richard Wright, *Black Boy*

BETTER THAN ONE

■

British satirist Evelyn Waugh had a low opinion of literary collaboration: "I never could understand how two men can write a book together," he once said. "To me that's like three people getting together to have a baby."

In 1969, a group of people did indeed get together to produce an enormous literary baby. A man named Mike McGrady decided, as a literary lark, to put together a syndicate of some twenty people to create the worst sex novel ever committed to paper. McGrady's instructions to his consortium: "There will be an unremitting emphasis on sex. Also true excellence in writing will be blue-penciled into oblivion."

Each member of the group wrote a chapter independently of the others, and what emerged was a titillating bodice-ripper titled *Naked Came the Stranger,* published with the name of a nonexistent Penelope Ashe as its lone author. Even after the hoax was revealed, the book continued to sell well, chalking up an astonishing 100,000 copies in hardcover, proving something about the American appetite for pulp sex.

Seldom do we find a collaboration of this magnitude, but some authors (Richard Lederer and Michael Gilleland, for example) have found that "two are better than one," as we learn in the Book of Ecclesiastes (4:9). Match each work with its tandem or trio of authors:

1. *The Communist Manifesto* — Maxwell Anderson and Laurence Stallings

2. *Deacon Brodie* — Francis Beaumont and John Fletcher

3. *The Federalist Papers* — Samuel Taylor Coleridge and William Wordsworth

4. *The Gilded Age* — Joseph Conrad and Ford Madox Ford

5. *Gorboduc* — Charles Dickens and Wilkie Collins

6. *The Inheritors* — John Fletcher and William Shakespeare

7. *Is Sex Necessary?* — Alexander Hamilton, John Jay, and James Madison

8. *Letters from Iceland* — George S. Kaufman and Moss Hart

9. *Lyrical Ballads* — Fletcher Knebel and Charles W. Bailey II

10. *The Man Who Came to Dinner* — Charles and Mary Lamb

11. *Mutiny on the Bounty* — William J. Lederer and Eugene L. Burdick

12. *Philaster* — Louis MacNeice and W. H. Auden

13. *Seven Days in May* — Karl Marx and Frederick Engels

14. *The Two Noble Kinsmen* — Charles Nordhoff and James Norman Hall

15. *Tales from Shakespeare* — Thomas Norton and Thomas Sackville

16. *The Ugly American*   Robert Louis Stevenson
                                         and W. E. Henley
17. *What Price Glory?*   Mark Twain and Charles
                                         Dudley Warner
18. *The Wreck of the Golden Mary*   E. B. White and James
                                         Thurber

"The isms go; the isms die; art remains," wrote Vladimir
Nabokov. "The moment a thing becomes an 'ism,' it is already
false," echoed Isaac Bashevis Singer. To which literary groups or
movements did these writers belong?:

19. William S. Burroughs, Lawrence Ferlinghetti, Allen Ginsberg, Jack Kerouac, Gary Snyder

20. Margaret Fuller, Bronson Alcott, Ralph Waldo Emerson,
Henry David Thoreau

21. E. M. Forster, Lytton Strachey, Virginia Woolf

22. William Wordsworth, Samuel Taylor Coleridge, Robert
Southey

23. Alexander Woolcott, Dorothy Parker, Robert Benchley,
George S. Kaufman

24. Émile Zola, Stephen Crane, Frank Norris, Theodore
Dreiser, James T. Farrell

25. Amy Lowell, Ezra Pound, H.D.

26. Dante Gabriel Rossetti, Algernon Swinburne, George
Meredith

27. Langston Hughes, Countee Cullen, Claude McKay

28. John Donne, George Herbert, Abraham Cowley

29. Richard Lovelace, Thomas Carew, Sir John Suckling

30. John Osborne, Kingsley Amis, John Wain

31. Allen Tate, John Crowe Ransom, Robert Penn Warren

32. C. S. Lewis, J.R.R. Tolkien

33. W. H. Auden, C. Day-Lewis, Stephen Spender

34. Eugene Ionesco, Samuel Beckett, Edward Albee

35. John Henry Newman, E. B. Pusey, John Keble

In Victorian England appeared a very proper and prissy volume, *Lady Gough's Book of Etiquette*. Among Lady Gough's social pronouncements was the stricture that under no circumstances should books written by male authors be placed on shelves next to books written by "authoresses." Married writers, however, such as Robert and Elizabeth Barrett Browning, could be placed together without impropriety.

Literary conjugation has been achieved by a number of husbands and wives, including Will and Ariel Durant (*The Story of Civilization*), Scott and Helen Nearing (*Living the Good Life*), and Colette and her husband Willy (the *Claudine* books). William Butler Yeats claimed that much of his book *Visions* was dictated by ghosts to his wife, the spiritualist medium Georgie Hyde Lees. (When asked if he had ever seen these spirits, Yeats replied that he hadn't, but he had *smelled* them.)

Match these literary husbands and literary wives:

Richard Aldington	Joan Didion
Thomas Carlyle	Hilda Doolittle
Raymond Carver	Louise Erdrich
Michael Dorris	Mary Ann Evans
John Gregory Dunne	Tess Gallagher
Donald Hall	Jane Kenyon
Ted Hughes	Mary McCarthy
Henry Kuttner	C. L. Moore
George Henry Lewes	Sylvia Plath
Sinclair Lewis	Jean Stafford
Robert Lowell	Dorothy Thompson
Edmund Wilson	Jane Welsh

ANSWERS

1. Karl Marx and Frederick Engels 2. Robert Louis Stevenson and W. E. Henley 3. Alexander Hamilton, John Jay, and James Madison 4. Mark Twain and Charles Dudley Warner 5. Thomas

Norton and Thomas Sackville 6. Joseph Conrad and Ford Madox Ford 7. E. B. White and James Thurber 8. Louis Mac-Neice and W. H. Auden 9. Samuel Taylor Coleridge and William Wordsworth 10. George S. Kaufman and Moss Hart

11. Charles Nordhoff and James Norman Hall 12. Francis Beaumont and John Fletcher 13. Fletcher Knebel and Charles W. Bailey II 14. John Fletcher and William Shakespeare 15. Charles and Mary Lamb 16. William J. Lederer and Eugene L. Burdick 17. Maxwell Anderson and Laurence Stallings 18. Charles Dickens and Wilkie Collins

19. Beat Generation 20. Transcendentalists 21. the Bloomsbury Group 22. Lake Poets 23. Algonquin Round Table 24. Naturalists 25. Imagists 26. Pre-Raphaelite Brotherhood 27. Harlem Renaissance poets 28. Metaphysical poets 29. Cavalier poets 30. Angry Young Men 31. Fugitive poets (also Agrarians) 32. Inklings 33. Marxist poets 34. Absurdists 35. The Oxford Movement

Richard Aldington and Hilda Doolittle; Thomas Carlyle and Jane Welsh; Raymond Carver and Tess Gallagher; Michael Dorris and Louise Erdrich; John Gregory Dunne and Joan Didion; Donald Hall and Jane Kenyon; Ted Hughes and Sylvia Plath; Henry Kuttner and C. L. Moore; George Henry Lewes and Mary Ann Evans; Sinclair Lewis and Dorothy Thompson; Robert Lowell and Jean Stafford; Edmund Wilson and Mary McCarthy

SUPER SLEUTHS

■

Arthur Conan Doyle wanted to give his fictional detective an outlandish first name and thought seriously about Sherrinford. Ultimately, the doctor turned author settled on the Christian name Sherlock, after a Yorkshire bowler named Mordecai Sherlock, against whom he had played cricket.

After seriously considering the last name of Hope, suggested by a whaling ship named the *Hope,* Doyle chose that of a much-admired American writer of the time, Oliver Wendell Holmes. A distinguished, brilliant, and multitalented pioneer in medicine and criminal psychology, Oliver Wendell was the perfect prototype for Doyle's consulting detective. That's why the world's most famous fictional sleuth isn't known as Sherrinford Hope.

Dashiell Hammett, on the other hand, gave his most famous creation his own first name, which was Sam, as in Samuel Dashiell Hammett. That's why the classic hard-boiled detective in *The Maltese Falcon* isn't Dash Spade.

The word *sleuth* is a clipping of *sleuthhound,* the Scottish bloodhound noted for its dogged pursuit of game, suspects, or fugitives. Match each author in the left-hand column with his or her sleuth to the right:

Margery Allingham	Roderick Alleyn
Edmund Clerihew Bentley	Lew Archer
Earl Derr Biggers	Father Brown
John Dickson Carr	Albert Campion
Raymond Chandler	Brother Cadfael
Leslie Charteris	Steve Carella
G. K. Chesterton	Charlie Chan
Agatha Christie	Sergeant Cribb
Edmund Crispin	C. Auguste Dupin
Antonia Fraser	Dr. Gideon Fell
Emile Gaboriau	Gervase Fen
Erle Stanley Gardner	Alan Grant
Sue Grafton	Cordelia Gray
Martha Grimes	Mike Hammer
P.D. James	Richard Jury
Harry Kemelman	Monsieur Lecoq
Peter Lovesey	Inspector Maigret
John D. MacDonald	Philip Marlowe
Ross Macdonald	Miss Jane Marple
Ngaio Marsh	Perry Mason
Ed McBain	Travis McGee
Sara Paretsky	Kinsey Millhone
Ellis Peters	Hercule Poirot
Edgar Allan Poe	The Saint (Simon Templar)
Dorothy Sayers	Jemima Shore
Georges Simenon	Rabbi David Small
Mickey Spillane	Philip Trent
Rex Stout	Philo Vance
Josephine Tey	V. I. Warshawski
S. S. Van Dine	Lord Peter Wimsey
	Nero Wolfe

ANSWERS

Margery Allingham—Albert Campion; Edmund Clerihew Bentley—Philip Trent; Earl Derr Biggers—Charlie Chan; John Dickson Carr—Dr. Gideon Fell; Raymond Chandler—Philip Marlowe; Leslie Charteris—The Saint (Simon Templar); G. K. Chesterton—Father Brown; Agatha Christie—Miss Jane Marple, Hercule Poirot; Edmund Crispin—Gervase Fen; Antonia Fraser—Jemima Shore

Emile Gaboriau—Monsieur Lecoq; Erle Stanley Gardner—Perry Mason; Sue Grafton—Kinsey Millhone; Martha Grimes—Richard Jury; P. D. James—Cordelia Gray; Harry Kemelman—Rabbi David Small; Peter Lovesey—Sergeant Cribb; John D. MacDonald—Travis McGee; Ross Macdonald—Lew Archer; Ngaio Marsh—Roderick Alleyn

Ed McBain—Steve Carella; Sara Paretsky—V. I. Warshawski; Ellis Peters—Brother Cadfael; Edgar Allan Poe—C. Auguste Dupin; Dorothy Sayers—Lord Peter Wimsey; Georges Simenon—Inspector Maigret; Mickey Spillane—Mike Hammer; Rex Stout—Nero Wolfe; Josephine Tey—Alan Grant; S. S. Van Dine—Philo Vance

TITLE MATCH

∎

H. Rider was Haggard, but Thomas was Hardy.

Oscar was Wilde, but Thornton was Wilder.

Dame May was Whitty, but John Greenleaf was Whittier.

As we come to the end of the "Authors" section of this book, let's have some pun fun with the last names of famous writers.

The trouble with literature is that authors write the wrong books. Sure, Allen Ginsberg's *Howl* is a great poem, but it should have been written by Saul Bellow. Then the book jacket would read, "*Howl*, by Bellow."

Kurt Vonnegut's most famous novel should have come from the mind of Eldridge Cleaver so the title page would announce "*Slaughterhouse-Five*, by Cleaver."

Flowers for Algernon, by Daniel Keyes, should have been written by Judy Blume or John Lyly, while Keyes himself should have written "The Rape of the Lock," by Alexander Pope, who should have written Willa Cather's *Death Comes for the Archbishop*.

Now that you have the idea, use the parenthesized first names as clues to indicate the last name of the author who should have written each of the works listed. Then identify the real author:

1. *Across the River and into the Trees*, by (Robert)_____
2. *The Agony and the Ecstasy*, by (Tom)_____ and (Frank)_____
3. *The Big Money*, by (Stephen)_____
4. *The Birds*, by (Stephen)_____
5. *The Chocolate Wars*, by (Walt)_____
6. *The Deerslayer*, by (Pearl)_____
7. "Elegy Written in a Country Churchyard," by (Anne)_____
8. *An Enemy of the People*, by (Daniel)_____
9. *Fahrenheit 451*, by (Christopher)_____
10. *Fear of Flying*, by (Noël)_____.
11. *Finnegan's Wake*, by (Robert P. Tristram)_____
12. "Fire and Ice," by (Robert)_____ and (C. P.)_____
13. *The Genius*, by (Christopher)_____
14. *Giles Goat-Boy*, by (Thomas)_____
15. *The Great Gatsby*, by (Andrew)_____
16. *Green Eggs and Ham*, by (Francis)_____
17. *Hans Brinker: or The Silver Skates*, by (Xaviera)_____
18. *The Horse's Mouth*, by (Joyce Carol)_____
19. *The House of the Dead*, by (Robert)_____
20. *Hotel*, by (James)_____
21. "I Sing the Body Electric," by (Isaac)_____
22. *The Joy of Sex*, by (e. e.)_____
23. *The Jungle*, by (William)_____
24. *King Solomon's Mines*, by (Oliver)_____
25. *Like Water for Chocolate*, by (O.)_____
26. *Literary Trivia*, by (William)_____
27. *Looking Backward*, by (Matthew)_____
28. *Looking for Mr. Goodbar*, by (John)_____
29. *Maggie, a Girl of the Streets*, by (Anthony)_____
30. *The Magic Barrel*, by (James Fenimore)_____
31. *The Man with the Golden Gun*, by (Neville)_____
32. *My Left Foot*, by (John)_____
33. "The Necklace," by (The Venerable)_____
34. *On the Beach*, by (George)_____

35. *Paradise Lost*, by (Lillian)_____
36. *The Pigman*, by (Sir John)_____
37. *The Plains of Passage*, by (Günter)_____
38. *Postcards From the Edge*, by (Norman)_____
39. *Rabbit, Run*, by (Robert Penn)_____
40. *A River Runs Through It*, by (Gwendolyn)_____
41. *Robinson Crusoe*, by (Nancy)_____
42. *The Snake Pit*, by (Franz)_____
43. "Song of Myself," by (Isaac Bashevis)_____
44. *The Sun Also Rises*, by (Amy)_____
45. *Tales of Robin Hood*, by (Robert)_____
46. *A Taste of Honey*, by (Margaret)_____
47. *The Voyeur*, by (Samuel)_____
48. *The Wealth of Nations*, by (Adrienne)_____
49. *What Makes Sammy Run?* by (Jonathan)_____
50. *White Fang*, by (Tom)_____

Stretching the appeal of authorial appellations even further, we can come up with a list of writers, from antiquity to the present, and the sports their last names suggest. For example, Henry Fielding, Richard Steele, Honoré de *Balz*ac, and the dean of them all, Homer, should have been baseball writers.

Sharpen your pun cells again. Using the first and middle names as clues, match each sport with the punderful last names of authors:

Tennis:

51. Miguel de_____
52. Richard_____
53. Robert W._____
54. George Gordon, Lord_____
55. Kurt_____
56. Ivy Compton_____
57. Alfred, Lord_____

Track:

58. Jonathan_____
59. John_____
60. John Crowe_____
61. Howard_____

Bowling:
62. Mickey_____   64. Harold_____
63. Beryl_____   65. Malcolm_____

Horse racing:
66. Walter_____   68. MacKinlay_____
67. Joyce Carol_____   69. Stephen Vincent_____

Football:
70. Joyce_____   72. John Dos_____
71. Robert_____

Riflery:
73. John_____   76. Kingsley_____
74. Nevil_____   77. Jean_____
75. Robert_____   78. The Venerable_____

Skiing:
79. C. P._____   82. Robert_____
80. James_____   83. Frederick_____
81. Samuel Taylor_____

Golf:
84. Sara_____   85. Graham_____

Crew:
86. Percy Bysshe_____   90. Iris_____
87. George_____   91. Lawrence_____
88. Harper_____   92. George_____
89. Marianne_____   93. Henry David_____

Basketball:
94. Francis Scott_____ 96. John_____
95. Henry Wadsworth_____

Rodeo:

97. Thomas_____   99. Pearl_____
98. Noël_____   100. Albert_____

ANSWERS

1. Bridges (Ernest Hemingway) 2. Paine and Lovejoy (Irving Stone) 3. Spender (John Dos Passos) 4. Hawking (Daphne du Maurier) 5. Whitman (Robert Cormier)

6. Buck (James Fenimore Cooper) 7. Sexton (Thomas Gray) 8. Defoe (Henrik Ibsen) 9. Frye (who actually did write *The Lady's Not for Burning*) (Ray Bradbury) 10. Coward (Erica Jong)

11. Coffin (James Joyce) 12. Burns and Snow (Robert Frost, which isn't bad) 13. Smart (Theodore Dreiser) 14. Kyd (John Barth) 15. Marvell (F. Scott Fitzgerald)

16. Bacon (Dr. Seuss) 17. Hollander (Mary Mapes Dodge) 18. Oates (Joyce Cary) 19. Graves (Fyodor Dostoevsky) 20. Hilton (Arthur Hailey)

21. Watts (Walt Whitman) 22. cummings (Alex Comfort, which is pretty good in itself) 23. Shakespeare (Upton Sinclair) 24. Goldsmith (H. Rider Haggard) 25. Henry (Laura Esquivel)

26. Wordsworth (Richard Lederer and Michael Gilleland) 27. Prior (Edward Bellamy) 28. Hersey (Judith Rossner) 29. Trollope (Stephen Crane) 30. Cooper (Bernard Malamud)

31. Shute (Ian Fleming) 32. Bunyan (Shane Connaughton and Jim Sheridan) 33. Bede (Guy de Maupassant) 34. Sand (Nevil Shute) 35. Hellman (John Milton)

36. Suckling (Paul Zindel) 37. Grass (Jean Auel) 38. Mailer (Carrie Fisher) 39. Warren (John Updike) 40. Brooks (Norman Maclean)

41. Friday (Daniel Defoe) 42. Boas (Sigrid Undset) 43. Singer (Walt Whitman) 44. Tan (Ernest Hemingway) 45. Sherwood (folk sources)

46. Mead (Shelagh Delaney) 47. Pepys (Alain Robbe-Grillet)

48. Rich (Adam Smith) 49. Swift (Budd Schulberg) 50. Wolfe (Jack London)

Tennis: 51. *Cerv*antes 52. *Love*lace 53. Service 54. *B*yron 55. Vonne*gut* 56. Bur*nett* 57. *Tenny*son

Track: 58. Swift 59. Bunyan 60. Ransom 61. Fast

Bowling: 62. Spil*lane* 63. *Mark*ham 64. *Pint*er 65. X

Horse racing: 66. de la Mare 67. Oates 68. Kantor 69. Ben*ét*

Football: 70. Cary 71. Bloch 72. *Pass*os

Riflery: 73. *Gun*ther 74. Shute 75. Bolt 76. Amis 77. *Coc*teau 78. Bede

Skiing: 79. Snow 80. *Hil*ton 81. Cole*ridge* 82. Frost 83. Pohl

Golf: 84. *Teas*dale 85. Greene

Crew: 86. *Shell*ey 87. Crabbe 88. Lee 89. Moore 90. Mur*doch* 91. Sterne 92. *Or*well 93. Tho*reau*

Basketball: 94. Key 95. Longfellow 96. Fowles

Rodeo: 97. *Bull*finch 98. *Cow*ard 99. Buck 100. Ca*mus*

THE FINAL CHAPTER

■

When the book of life ends, some men and women deliver closing lines that are recorded for posterity. Not surprisingly, some of the most famous of last words have been uttered by writers, creatively garrulous to the very end.

The Irish playwright Oscar Wilde, always one to turn a clever phrase, called for champagne and quipped, "I am dying as I have lived, beyond my means." Welsh poet Dylan Thomas, who also put the quart before the hearse, slurred, "I've had eighteen straight whiskeys. I think this is a record." And then he died.

German poet Heinrich Heine proclaimed, "God will pardon me; it's his profession." Oliver Goldsmith was more cynical. Dying from a surfeit of James's Powders, a preparation he was expressly forbidden to take, he was asked if his conscience was clear. His last utterance: "No, it is not."

When asked if he had made his peace with God, Henry David Thoreau said, just before he died, "I was not aware that we had ever quarreled." As she lay dying of cancer, the American expatriate writer Gertrude Stein asked her friend Alice B. Toklas, "What is the answer?" When Ms. Toklas, overcome by grief, could not respond, the writer spoke again: "In that case, what is the question?" When H. G. Wells was on his deathbed, his friends and relatives gathered around and tried to extract some famous last words. The great writer whispered with some impatience, "Can't you see I'm busy dying!"

The journey to "that undiscovered country from whose bourn no traveler returns" often reveals a lot about a person's life. Identify each author from the description of his or her denouement:

1. This Greek playwright is said to have died of a skull fracture when an eagle dropped a tortoise on his bald head, mistaking it for a rock.

2. This author of *Le Morte d'Arthur* spent the last twenty years of his life in prison.

3. This British Lord Chancellor, who wrote *Utopia,* was imprisoned and executed for refusing to sign Henry VIII's oath of supremacy.

4. Although desperately ill, this French actor and dramatist insisted on going onstage so as not to let down the rest of the company. When the play was over, he had to be carried home, where he died shortly afterward of a burst blood vessel in his throat.

5. This London man of letters published an annotated edition of *The Plays of Shakespeare.* Years later he was buried in the Poets' Corner of Westminster Abbey at the foot of Shakespeare's statue.

6. This English Romantic poet sailed to Greece to fight in its war for independence. There he became ill with a fever brought on by getting very hot from riding and then being drenched in a thunderstorm while he was rowing an open boat across a lagoon. The poet's death, at thirty-six, created a sensation throughout the literary world.

7. When he was twenty-three, this Romantic poet prophetically wrote:

> *When I have fears that I may cease to be*
> *Before my pen had glean'd my teeming brain,*
> *Before high piled books in charactery*
> *Hold like rich garners the full-ripened grain.*

A year later he stopped writing because of poor health and died at twenty-five, nevertheless leaving a priceless legacy of luminous poetry. He wished for no name or inscription on his grave, but simply the words "Here lies one whose name was writ in water."

8. This American writer of short stories and poems spent his last days stumbling into Baltimore polling places and casting ballots for drinks. While preparing for his wedding, he was found wandering deliriously near a saloon and died, at the age of forty, four days later.

9. This American humorist predicted that he would die the same year that Halley's Comet visited (1910), and he did. The inscription on his gravestone in Elmira, New York, preserves one of his most famous quotations: "The reports of my death are greatly exaggerated."

10. This American writer and war correspondent succumbed to tuberculosis at the age of twenty-nine.

11. In 1904, this Russian playwright and short story writer died in Germany right after offering a toast to his wife. His body was returned to Moscow in a refrigerated railway car marked "For Oysters."

12. This Russian novelist died in Astapovo in 1910, trying to escape from his wife. As he lay on his deathbed, he refused to be converted to the Russian Orthodox Church. "Even in the valley of the shadow of death," he told the priest, "two and two do not make six."

13. This American satirist disappeared somewhere in the Mexican desert in 1913. His last letter, sent from Chihuahua, Mexico, reads, "If you hear of my being stood up against a Mexican wall and shot to rags, please know that it is a pretty good way to depart this life. It beats old age, disease, or falling down the cellar stairs." No one knows if he was killed fighting beside Pancho Villa or died at the hands of Mexican bandits.

14. This American poet wrote the poem "I Have a Rendez-vous With Death" and then was killed in 1916 fighting for the French Foreign Legion.

15. In 1936, the greatest poet and playwright of modern Spain was shot in his native city of Grenada by Franco's henchmen.

16. This American playwright requested this inscription on his tombstone: "There is something to be said for being dead."

17. This American writer was remembered by this memorial in the lobby of the Baltimore *Sun,* a newspaper with which he was long associated: "If after I depart this vale you ever remember me and have thought to please my ghost, forgive some sinner and wink your eye at some homely girl."

18. This American writer of fiction committed suicide by firing a shotgun into his head, the same weapon his father had used on himself.

19. and 20. These two American confessional poets, who were students together and friends after, both committed suicide. The first died at the age of thirty after putting her head in an oven and turning on the gas, the second at the age of forty-six after gassing herself in her garage.

21. In 1969 at the age of thirty-two, this American writer committed suicide in despair over his inability to find a publisher for *A Confederacy of Dunces.* It was published posthumously eleven years after.

22. This French philosopher succumbed to voluntary starvation in 1943 in London, after refusing to eat more than the rations allowed in occupied France.

23. This American poet has for the epitaph on his gravestone a line from one of his poems: "I had a lover's quarrel with the world."

24. This Elizabethan playwright reputedly died on the same day, and in the same month, that he was born. His death was reported thusly: "_____, Drayton, and Ben Jhonson had a merry meeting, and itt seems drank too hard, for_____died of a feavour there contracted."

25. After many early successes, this Elizabethan playwright died, when he was but twenty-nine, of stab wounds above the

right eye. Some scholars believe that he was killed in a tavern brawl in a dispute over the bill. Others conjecture that he was the victim of political assassination. Still a third theory holds that the scene at the inn was actually a plot to produce the rumor of his death, enabling him to go on a secret mission of espionage.

26. During his last two years, this American writer of fiction drank Coca-Cola by the case instead of the alcohol that had wrecked his life. Drained of energy, he wrote his final novel, *The Last Tycoon,* in bed, but died before its completion. No one came to his funeral, prompting Dorothy Parker to say, "Poor son of a bitch," a quotation from his most famous book.

27. This Russian author died of "an artery burst in the lungs," just as he had actually dictated in a third-person account of his own death. More than 100,000 people spontaneously lined the streets at his funeral, the largest funeral procession for any writer in history.

28. Writing about moral issues of universal importance, this French existential novelist and essayist gained worldwide attention. At forty-six and at the height of his fame, the car in which he was riding left the road and slammed into a tree. He died instantly of a skull fracture.

ANSWERS

1. Aeschylus 2. Sir Thomas Malory 3. Sir Thomas More 4. Molière 5. Samuel Johnson 6. Lord Byron 7. John Keats 8. Edgar Allan Poe 9. Mark Twain 10. Stephen Crane

11. Anton Chekhov 12. Leo Tolstoy 13. Ambrose Bierce 14. Alan Seeger 15. Federico García Lorca 16. Eugene O'Neill 17. H. L. Mencken 18. Ernest Hemingway 19. Sylvia Plath 20. Anne Sexton

21. John Kennedy Toole 22. Simone Weil 23. Robert Frost 24. William Shakespeare 25. Christopher Marlowe 26. F. Scott Fitzgerald 27. Fyodor Dostoevsky 28. Albert Camus

·Titles·

ALLITERATURE

■

Alliteration is the occurrence within a line or phrase of words having the same initial sound. It's a device that many writers employ to create a treasure trove of tried-and-true, bread-and-butter, bigger-and-better, bright-eyed and bushy-tailed, do-or-die, footloose-and-fancy-free, larger-than-life, cream-of-the-crop titles. Using the clues of author and alliterated letter, identify the following alliterary works whose titles employ "apt alliteration's artful aid":

1. Booth Tarkington (A)
2. Hervey Allen (A)
3. John Dryden (A)
4. Herman Melville (B)
5. Richard Wright (B)
6. Brendan Behan (B)
7. Anna Sewell (B)
8. Jonathan Swift (B)
9. Charles Dickens (C)
10. Rudyard Kipling (C)
11. O. Henry (C, K)
12. Kurt Vonnegut (C)
13. T.S. Eliot (C)
14. Cleveland Amory (C)
15. George Bernard Shaw (D)
16. Stephen Vincent Benét (D)
17. George Eliot (D)
18. Ambrose Bierce (D)
19. John Steinbeck (E)
20. Erica Jong (F)
21. Mary O'Hara (F)
22. F. Scott Fitzgerald (G)

23. Gerard Manley Hopkins (G)
24. the Pearl Poet (G)
25. George Bernard Shaw (H)
26. John Patrick (H)
27. William Wordsworth (I)
28. Samuel Taylor Coleridge (K)
29. William Shakespeare (L)
30. Irving Stone (L)
31. Sir Walter Scott (L)
32. Eugene O'Neill (L)
33. Frank Harris (L)
34. A. R. Gurney (L)
35. John Steinbeck (M)
36. Thomas Mann (M)
37. Herman Wouk (M)
38. Nathaniel Hawthorne (M)
39. Mikhail Bulgakov (M)
40. Eugene O'Neill (M)
41. Charles Dickens (N)
42. William Morris (N)
43. Jane Austen (P)
44. Charles Dickens (P)
45. Grace Metalious (P)
46. James Barrie (P)
47. Mark Twain (P)
48. John Bunyan (P)
49. Robert Browning (P)
50. Edgar Allan Poe (P)
51. Kurt Vonnegut (P)
52. Jean Auel (P)
53. William Langland (P)
54. John Updike (R)
55. Tobias Smollett (R)
56. Sir Walter Scott (R)
57. Arthur Conan Doyle (S)
58. Richard Brinsley Sheridan (S)
59. Joseph Conrad (S)
60. Jane Austen (S)
61. Rachel Carson (S)
62. Simone de Beauvoir (S)
63. T. H. White (S)
64. J.R.R. Tolkien (T)
65. Nathaniel Hawthorne (T)
66. Jonathan Swift (T)
67. Kenneth Grahame (W)
68. H. G. Wells (W)
69. Herman Wouk (W)
70. Wilkie Collins (W)

As long as you're being so alliterate, identify the alliteratively named authors who wrote the following works:

71. *Mother Courage and Her Children* (B)
72. *The Quare Fellow* (B)
73. *Color* (C)
74. *The Wife of His Youth* (C)
75. *Moll Flanders* (D)
76. *Rebecca* (D)
77. *People Like Us* (D)

78. *Fried Green Tomatoes at the Whistle Stop Cafe* (F)
79. *Day of the Jackal* (F)
80. *The Power and the Glory* (G)
81. *The Tin Drum* (G)
82. *Siddhartha* (H)
83. *Deutschland, Deutschland* (H)
84. *Ulysses* (J)
85. *From Here to Eternity* (J)
86. *The Bastard* (J)
87. *The Autobiography of an Ex-Colored Man* (J)
88. *Sometimes a Great Notion* (K)
89. *How the West Was Won* (L)
90. *Gone with the Wind* (M)
91. *"Baseball and Writing"* (M)
92. *The Group* (M)
93. *Understanding Media* (M)
94. *Growing Up in New Guinea* (M)
95. *Essais* (M)
96. *Chronicles of Wasted Time* (M)
97. *Styles of Radical Will* (S)
98. *Master of the Game* (S)
99. *Leaves of Grass* (W)
100. *Lyrical Ballads* (W)

ANSWERS

1. *Alice Adams* 2. *Anthony Adverse* 3. *Absalom and Achitophel* 4. *Billy Budd* 5. *Black Boy* 6. *Borstal Boy* 7. *Black Beauty* 8. *The Battle of the Books* 9. *A Christmas Carol* 10. *Captains Courageous* 11. *Cabbages and Kings* 12. *Cat's Cradle* 13. *The Confidential Clerk* 14. *The Cat and the Curmudgeon* 15. *The Devil's Disciple, The Doctor's Dilemma* 16. *"The Devil and Daniel Webster"* 17. *Daniel Deronda* 18. *The Devil's Dictionary* 19. *East of Eden* 20. *Fear of Flying*

21. *My Friend Flicka* 22. *The Great Gatsby* 23. *"God's Grandeur"* 24. *Sir Gawain and the Green Knight* 25. *Heartbreak House* 26. *The Hasty Heart* 27. *"Intimations of Immortality"* 28. *"Kubla Khan"* 29. *Love's Labour's Lost* 30. *Lust for Life*

31. *The Lady of the Lake* 32. *Lazarus Laughed* 33. *My Life and Loves* 34. *Love Letters* 35. *Of Mice and Men* 36. *The Magic Mountain; Mario and the Magician* 37. *Marjorie Morningstar* 38. *Mosses*

from an Old Manse 39. *The Master and Margarita* 40. *Marco Millions, A Moon for the Misbegotten*

41. *Nicholas Nickleby* 42. *News from Nowhere* 43. *Pride and Prejudice* 44. *The Pickwick Papers* 45. *Peyton Place* 46. *Peter Pan* 47. *The Prince and the Pauper* 48. *The Pilgrim's Progress* 49. *Pippa Passes* and "The Pied Piper of Hamelin" 50. "The Pit and the Pendulum"

51. *Player Piano* 52. *The Plains of Passage* 53. *Piers Plowman* 54. *Rabbit, Run; Rabbit is Rich; Rabbit Redux* 55. *Roderick Random* 56. *Rob Roy* 57. *A Study in Scarlet* 58. *The School for Scandal* 59. "The Secret Sharer" 60. *Sense and Sensibility*

61. *The Silent Spring* 62. *The Second Sex* 63. *The Sword in the Stone* 64. *The Two Towers* 65. *Twice-Told Tales* 66. *A Tale of a Tub* 67. *The Wind in the Willows* 68. *The War of the Worlds* 69. *The Winds of War* 70. *The Woman in White*

71. Bertolt Brecht 72. Brendan Behan 73. Countee Cullen 74. Charles W. Chestnutt 75. Daniel Defoe 76. Daphne du Maurier 77. Dominick Dunne 78. Fannie Flagg 79. Frederic Forsyth 80. Graham Greene

81. Günter Grass 82. Hermann Hesse 83. Heinrich Heine 84. James Joyce 85. James Jones 86. John Jakes 87. James Weldon Johnson 88. Ken Kesey 89. Louis L'Amour 90. Margaret Mitchell

91. Marianne Moore 92. Mary McCarthy 93. Marshall McLuhan 94. Margaret Mead 95. Michel de Montaigne 96. Malcolm Muggeridge 97. Susan Sontag 98. Sidney Sheldon 99. Walt Whitman 100. William Wordsworth

THE SPECTRUM OF LITERATURE

■

British poet and satirist Hilaire Belloc wrote as his epitaph:

> *When I am dead, I hope it may be said,*
> *"His sins were scarlet, but his books were read."*

Belloc is little-read today, alas, but, picking up on his waggish pun, we note that a number of books are black and white and read all over—and yellow and gold and silver and blue and purple and scarlet and green and orange and gray.

In the spectrum of literature, colors play an important role in the names of books. In Bruce Catton's classic study of the Civil War, *The Blue and the Gray,* the colors, of course, signify the two sides in the conflict. Less obvious is *The Red and the Black,* in which Stendhal creates a psychological study of the self-absorbed Julien Sorel. The two colors in the novel's title represent the military and the clergy, the two paths open to a young man of the hero's class.

We'll pull out the red carpet and award you a blue ribbon and gold star if you can get your gray matter to identify the colorful titles created by the following authors:

Black:
1. Lorene Cary
2. Jean Genet
3. Edgar Allan Poe

4. Anna Sewell
5. Richard Wright

White:
6. Wilkie Collins
7. Don DeLillo
8. Joan Didion
9. Ernest Hemingway
10. Sarah Orne Jewett

11. D. H. Lawrence
12. Jack London
13. Herman Melville
14. D. M. Thomas
15. John Webster

Red:
16. Stephen Crane
17. Tom Clancy
18. Arthur Conan Doyle

19. Edgar Allan Poe
20. John Steinbeck
21. James Jones

Yellow:
22. Charlotte P. Gilman
23. Aldous Huxley

24. Fred Gipson

Gold:
25. Ray Bradbury
26. Sir James George Frazer
27. Carson McCullers

28. Edgar Allan Poe
29. Henry James

Silver:
30. Mary Mapes Dodge

Blue:
31. Arthur Conan Doyle

32. Toni Morrison

Purple:
33. Alice Walker

34. Zane Grey

Scarlet:
35. Arthur Conan Doyle   37. Baroness Orczy
36. Nathaniel Hawthorne

Green:
38. Marc Connelly   43. Robin Moore
39. Fannie Flagg   44. Lucy Maud Montgomery
40. Ernest Hemingway   45. Dr. Seuss
41. W. H. Hudson   46. Charles Reich
42. Richard Llewellyn

Orange:
47. Anthony Burgess   48. Arthur Conan Doyle

Gray:
49. Oscar Wilde   50. Sloane Wilson

ANSWERS

1. *Black Ice* 2. *The Blacks* 3. "The Black Cat" 4. *Black Beauty*
5. *Black Boy*

6. *The Woman in White* 7. *White Noise* 8. *The White Album*
9. "Hills Like White Elephants" 10. "A White Heron" 11. *The White Peacock* 12. *White Fang* 13. *White Jacket* 14. *The White Hotel*
15. *The White Devil*

16. *The Red Badge of Courage* 17. *The Hunt for Red October; Red Storm Rising* 18. "The Red-Headed League" 19. "The Masque of the Red Death" 20. *The Red Pony* 21. *The Thin Red Line*

22. "The Yellow Wallpaper" 23. *Crome Yellow* 24. *Old Yeller*

25. *The Golden Apples of the Sun* 26. *The Golden Bough*
27. *Reflections in a Golden Eye* 28. "The Gold Bug" 29. *The Golden Bowl*

30. *Hans Brinker: or The Silver Skates*

31. "The Blue Carbuncle" 32. *The Bluest Eye*

33. *The Color Purple* 34. *Riders of the Purple Sage*

35. *A Study in Scarlet* 36. *The Scarlet Letter* 37. *The Scarlet Pimpernel*

38. *The Green Pastures* 39. *Fried Green Tomatoes at the Whistle Stop Cafe* 40. *The Green Hills of Africa* 41. *Green Mansions*
42. *How Green was My Valley* 43. *The Green Berets* 44. *Anne of Green Gables* 45. *Green Eggs and Ham* 46. *The Greening of America*

47. *A Clockwork Orange* 48. "The Five Orange Pips"

49. *The Picture of Dorian Gray* 50. *The Man in the Gray Flannel Suit*

THE BESTIARY

■

Animals are the main characters in much of world literature, and collections of these tales were often called bestiaries. This animated tradition stretches from Aesop's fables and the mock epic *Batrachomyomachia* (*Battle of the Frogs and Mice*), attributed to Homer, to modern works, such as George Orwell's *Animal Farm*, satirizing Russia under Stalin. Even when animals are not central characters, they roam the titles of books such as Tennessee Williams's *The Glass Menagerie*, Edward Albee's *Zoo Story*, Stephen King's *Pet Sematary*, and Barbara Kingsolver's *Animal Dreams*.

As Walt Whitman reminds us in "Song of Myself," we have much to learn from animals:

> *I think I could turn and live with animals,*
> *They are so placid and self contain'd,*
> *I stand and look at them long and long.*

The authors listed below have written works that cage mammals in their titles. Identify each title:

1. Jean Auel
2. John Barth
3. Michael Blake
4. William Blake

 5. Pierre Boulle
 6. Robert Burns
 7. Edgar Rice Burroughs
 8. Joyce Cary
 9. James Clavell
10. James Fenimore Cooper
11. Agatha Christie
12. Arthur Conan Doyle
13. T. S. Eliot
14. William Faulkner
15. Frederick Forsyth
16. James Goldman
17. Ernest Hebert
18. Robert Heinlein
19. Lillian Hellman
20. Hermann Hesse
21. Aldous Huxley
22. Eugene Ionesco
23. Henry James
24. Ben Jonson
25. Rudyard Kipling
26. C. S. Lewis
27. Jack London

28. Thomas Harris
29. Alistair MacLean
30. Norman Mailer
31. David Mamet
32. Larry McMurtry
33. Desmond Morris
34. Eugene O'Neill
35. George Orwell
36. Edgar Allan Poe
37. Bernard Pomerance
38. Katherine Anne Porter
39. Peter Shaffer
40. George Bernard Shaw
41. Irwin Shaw
42. Dodie Smith
43. John Steinbeck
44. Frank Stockton
45. Robert Stone
46. Dylan Thomas
47. John Updike
48. Kurt Vonnegut
49. Tennessee Williams
50. Frank Yerby

From Aristophanes' *The Birds* to John Grisham's best-selling *The Pelican Brief*, writers have sought out feathered friends to inspire names for their works. Using the authors' names as clues, identify works whose titles are for the birds:

51. Maya Angelou
52. Richard Bach
53. William Cullen Bryant

54. Geoffrey Chaucer
55. Anton Chekhov
56. Margaret Craven

57. T. S. Eliot
58. Anatole France
59. Paul Gallico
60. Dashiell Hammett
61. Thomas Hardy
62. Jack Higgins
63. Aldous Huxley
64. Henrik Ibsen
65. Henry James
66. Sarah Orne Jewett
67. John Keats
68. Ken Kesey
69. Jerzy Kosinski

70. D. H. Lawrence
71. Edward Lear
72. Harper Lee
73. Alistair MacLean
74. Colleen McCullough
75. Larry McMurtry
76. Sean O'Casey
77. Alan Paton
78. Edgar Allan Poe
79. Tom Robbins
80. Percy Bysshe Shelley
81. John Updike
82. Tennessee Williams

Emily Dickinson wrote a poem about "a narrow Fellow in the Grass" who never failed to make her feel a "Zero at the Bone." The poet never provided a title and avoided using the word *snake* in the poem so that her readers would have to guess the identity of the "Whip lash/Upbraiding in the Sun."

Other authors are not so coy and do identify their nonmammalian and nonavian subjects in their titles. Identify those titles for each of the following authors:

83. Aristophanes
84. Richard Brautigan
85. Robert Burns
86. Charles Dickens
87. John Donne
88. William Golding
89. D. H. Lawrence
90. Robert Merle
91. Frank Norris

92. Sigrid Undset
93. Edgar Allan Poe
94. Manuel Puig
95. Jean-Paul Sartre
96. Mark Twain
97. Nathanael West
98. Walt Whitman
99. Tennessee Williams
100. Philip Wylie

ANSWERS

1. *The Clan of the Cave Bear; The Valley of Horses; The Mammoth Hunters* 2. *Giles Goat-Boy* 3. *Dances with Wolves* 4. "The Tiger"; "The Lamb" 5. *Planet of the Apes* 6. "To a Mouse" 7. *Tarzan of the Apes* 8. *The Horse's Mouth* 9. *King Rat* 10. *The Deerslayer*

11. *The Mouse Trap* 12. "The Hound of the Baskervilles" 13. *Old Possum's Book of Practical Cats* 14. "The Bear" 15. *Day of the Jackal* 16. *The Lion In Winter* 17. *The Dogs of March* 18. *The Cat Who Walks Through Walls* 19. *The Little Foxes* 20. *Steppenwolf*

21. *Ape and Essence* 22. *The Rhinoceros* 23. "The Beast in the Jungle" 24. *Volpone, or The Fox* 25. "The Elephant's Child"; "How the Camel Got Its Hump"; "How the Leopard Got Its Spots"; "How the Rhino Got Its Skin" 26. *The Lion, the Witch, and the Wardrobe* 27. *The Sea-Wolf* 28. *Silence of the Lambs* 29. *Ice Station Zebra* 30. *The Deer Park*

31. *American Buffalo* 32. *Horseman, Pass By* 33. *The Naked Ape* 34. *The Hairy Ape* 35. "Shooting an Elephant" 36. "The Black Cat" 37. *The Elephant Man* 38. *Pale Horse, Pale Rider* 39. *Equus* 40. *Androcles and the Lion*

41. *The Young Lions* 42. *101 Dalmatians* 43. *Of Mice and Men; The Red Pony* 44. "The Lady or the Tiger" 45. *Dog Soldiers* 46. *Portrait of the Artist as a Young Dog* 47. *Rabbit, Run; Rabbit Redux; Rabbit is Rich* 48. *Welcome to the Monkey House; Cat's Cradle* 49. *Cat on a Hot Tin Roof* 50. *The Foxes of Harrow*

51. *I Know Why the Caged Bird Sings* 52. *Jonathan Livingston Seagull* 53. "To a Waterfowl" 54. *The Parliament of Fowls* 55. *The Sea Gull* 56. *I Heard the Owl Call My Name* 57. "Sweeney Among the Nightingales" 58. *Penguin Island* 59. *The Snow Goose* 60. *The Maltese Falcon*

61. "Darkling Thrush" 62. *The Eagle Has Flown; The Eagle Has Landed* 63. *After Many a Summer Dies the Swan* 64. *The Wild Duck* 65. *The Wings of the Dove* 66. "A White Heron" 67. "Ode to a Nightingale" 68. *One Flew Over the Cuckoo's Nest* 69. *The Painted Bird* 70. *The White Peacock*

71. "The Owl and the Pussy-Cat" 72. *To Kill a Mockingbird* 73. *Where Eagles Dare* 74. *The Thorn Birds* 75. *Lonesome Dove* 76. *Juno and the Paycock* 77. *Too Late the Phalarope* (A phalarope is a small seabird resembling a sandpiper.) 78. "The Raven" 79. *Still Life with Woodpecker* 80. "To a Skylark"

81. *Pigeon Feathers* 82. *Sweet Bird of Youth* 83. *The Frogs; The Wasps* 84. *Trout Fishing in America* 85. "To a Louse" 86. "The Cricket on the Hearth" 87. "The Flea" 88. *Lord of the Flies* 89. *The Plumed Serpent,* plus poems with animal titles 90. *Day of the Dolphin*

91. *The Octopus* 92. *The Snake Pit* 93. "The Gold Bug" 94. *The Kiss of the Spider Woman* 95. *The Flies* 96. "The Celebrated Jumping Frog of Calaveras County" 97. *Day of the Locust* 98. "A Noiseless Patient Spider" 99. *Night of the Iguana* 100. *Generation of Vipers*

VEGGING OUT

■

Cavalier poet Andrew Marvell wooed his "Coy Mistress" by promising that "my vegetable love should grow/Vaster than empires and more slow." Writers often pluck their titles from the plant kingdom, from Emmuska Orczy's *The Scarlet Pimpernel,* in which the pimpernel is actually an herb in the primrose family, to George Orwell's *Keep the Aspidistra Flying,* in which an aspidistra is an Asian plant of the lily family. Identify the herbs, flowers, fruits, vegetables, and plants growing in the titles of the cultivated books written by the following down-to-earth authors:

1. John Barth
2. Ray Bradbury
3. Richard Brautigan
4. Erskine Caldwell
5. Anton Chekhov
6. Umberto Eco
7. Louise Erdrich
8. William Faulkner
9. Fannie Flagg
10. Kenneth Grahame
11. Joanne Greenburg
12. Lorraine Hansberry
13. Nathaniel Hawthorne
14. Ernest Hemingway
15. Jean Kerr
16. Daniel Keyes
17. Joyce Kilmer
18. Stephen King
19. W. Somerset Maugham
20. Margaret Mead

21. O. Henry
22. Eugene O'Neill
23. J. D. Salinger
24. George Bernard Shaw
25. Betty Smith
26. John Steinbeck

27. Jean Toomer
28. Mark Twain
29. Joseph Wambaugh
30. Walt Whitman
31. Tennessee Williams
32. Paul Zindel

ANSWERS

1. *The Sot-Weed Factor* 2. *Dandelion Wine; The Golden Apples of the Sun* 3. *In Watermelon Sugar* 4. *Tobacco Road* 5. *The Cherry Orchard;* "Gooseberries" 6. *The Name of the Rose* 7. *The Beet Queen* 8. "A Rose for Emily"; *A Green Bough* 9. *Fried Green Tomatoes at the Whistle Stop Cafe* 10. *The Wind in the Willows*

11. *I Never Promised You a Rose Garden* 12. *A Raisin in the Sun* 13. *Mosses from an Old Manse* 14. *Across the River and into the Trees* 15. *Please Don't Eat the Daisies* 16. *Flowers for Algernon* 17. "Trees" 18. *Children of the Corn* 19. "The Lotus Eater" 20. *Blackberry Winter*

21. *Cabbages and Kings* 22. *Desire Under the Elms* 23. *The Catcher in the Rye* 24. *The Apple Cart* 25. *A Tree Grows in Brooklyn* 26. *The Grapes of Wrath* 27. *Cane* 28. *The Adventures of Huckleberry Finn* 29. *The Onion Field* 30. *Leaves of Grass*

31. *The Rose Tattoo; Twenty-Seven Wagons Full of Cotton* 32. *The Effect of Gamma Rays on Man-in-the-Moon Marigolds*

PLAYING THE NUMBERS GAME

■

When a number of books he had lent were not returned, Sir Walter Scott quipped, "My friends may not be good in mathematics, but they are excellent book-keepers." Authors are sometimes unmathematical, but the numbers they place in some of their titles are often significant to the stories themselves. In Ray Bradbury's *Fahrenheit 451,* for example, the title turns out to be the temperature at which book paper ignites, an important figure in a society that employs firemen not to save houses but to burn down houses—houses suspected of containing books.

Joseph Heller's *Catch-22* refers to a military regulation that keeps pilots flying one suicidal mission after another. ("That's some catch, that Catch-22," observes Yossarian. "It's the best there is," Doc Daneeka agrees.) The only way to be excused from such duty is to be declared insane, but asking to be excepted is proof of a rational mind and bars excuse. The number 22 rhythmically and symbolically captures the double duplicity of both the military code and the bizarre world that Heller shapes in his novel.

Using the name of each author (or source) and each embedded number, provide the title of each work:

1. Alexandr Solzhenitsyn (1)
2. Ken Kesey (1)
3. T. H. White (1)
4. William Shakespeare (2)
5. Charles Dickens (2)
6. Richard Henry Dana (2)
7. Alexandre Dumas (3)
8. Anton Chekhov (3)
9. John Dos Passos (3)
10. T. S. Eliot (4)
11. Arthur Conan Doyle (4)
12. Kurt Vonnegut (5)
13. Ernest Hemingway (5)
14. Arthur Conan Doyle (5)
15. Luigi Pirandello (6)
16. A. A. Milne (6)
17. W. Somerset Maugham (6)
18. Nathaniel Hawthorne (7)
19. Nicholas Meyer (7)
20. Aeschylus (7)
21. T. E. Lawrence (7)
22. Fletcher Knebel and
    Charles W. Bailey II (7)
23. Richard Wright (8)
24. John O'Hara (8)
25. J. D. Salinger (9)
26. Dorothy L. Sayers (9)
27. Agatha Christie (10)
28. John Reed (10)
29. William Shakespeare (12)
30. Reginald Rose (12)
31. Booth Tarkington (17)
32. Leon Uris (18)
33. A. E. Housman (21)
34. John Buchan (39)
35. John Dos Passos (42)
36. Thomas Pynchon (49)
37. Harold Robbins (79)
38. Jules Verne (80)
39. Helene Hanff (84)
40. Victor Hugo (93)
41. Gabriel García Márquez
    (100)
42. Dodie Smith (101)
43. Marquis de Sade (120)
44. Arthur Schlesinger
    (1,000)
45. Arabian folk tales (1,001)
46. Arthur C. Clarke (2,001)
47. Jules Verne (20,000)
48. Ernest Hemingway
    (50,000)
49. Mark Twain (1,000,000)
50. O. Henry (4,000,000)

One of the most enigmatic of number mysteries occurs in a text, not a title. What may well be the most famous of O. Henry's short stories, "The Gift of the Magi" (1906), begins with this sentence: "One dollar and eighty-seven cents. That was all. And sixty cents of it was in pennies."

Do we have here yet another creative but impractical author who has trouble with his math? It is, of course, impossible to make up $1.87 if sixty (rather than sixty-two) cents of it is in pennies.

But not so fast. Turns out that, in the United States, two- and three-cent pieces were struck during the late nineteenth century and remained in circulation for decades after. Thus, it would have been quite possible in O. Henry's America to have a dollar and eighty-seven cents that did not include any pennies.

ANSWERS

1. *One Day in the Life of Ivan Denisovich* 2. *One Flew Over the Cuckoo's Nest* 3. *The Once and Future King* 4. *Two Gentlemen of Verona; The Two Noble Kinsmen* (with John Fletcher) 5. *A Tale of Two Cities* 6. *Two Years Before the Mast* 7. *The Three Musketeers* 8. *The Three Sisters* 9. *Three Soldiers* 10. *Four Quartets*

11. "The Sign of Four" 12. *Slaughterhouse-Five* 13. *The Fifth Column* 14. "The Five Orange Pips" 15. *Six Characters In Search of an Author* 16. *Now We Are Six* 17. *The Moon and Sixpence* 18. *The House of the Seven Gables* 19. *The Seven-Per-Cent Solution* 20. *Seven Against Thebes*

21. *Seven Pillars of Wisdom* 22. *Seven Days in May* 23. *Eight Men* 24. *Butterfield 8* 25. *Nine Stories* 26. *The Nine Tailors* 27. *Ten Little Indians* 28. *Ten Days That Shook the World* 29. *Twelfth Night* 30. *Twelve Angry Men*

31. *Seventeen* 32. *Mila 18* 33. "When I was One-and-Twenty" 34. *The Thirty-Nine Steps* 35. *The 42nd Parallel* 36. *The Crying of Lot 49* 37. *79 Park Avenue* 38. *Around the World in Eighty Days* 39. *84, Charing Cross Road* 40. *Ninety-Three*

41. *One Hundred Years of Solitude* 42. *101 Dalmatians* 43. *One Hundred Twenty Days of Sodom* 44. *The Thousand Days* 45. *The Thousand and One Nights* 46. *2001: A Space Odyssey* 47. *Twenty Thousand Leagues under the Sea* 48. "Fifty Grand" 49. "The £1,000,000 Bank-Note" 50. *The Four Million*

TITLE SEARCH

∎

Master storyteller W. Somerset Maugham once revealed how he constructed his many titles: "A good title is apt, specific, attractive, new, and short." In addition to these recommended qualities, some famous titles possess intrigue by inviting us into the books they name so that we can find out what the title actually means.

For many readers, the title *One Flew Over the Cuckoo's Nest* seems to be no more than a casual reference to a children's folk rhyme. Others are drawn by the contradiction embedded in Ken Kesey's title into the eccentric, polarized world of the novel. Cuckoos do not build nests; they lay their eggs in the nests of other birds. The contradiction mirrors the central irrationality of the novel itself, in which the bars separating the sane and insane, saints and sinners, and watchers and watched waver and blur.

Answer each of the following questions to show how the meanings of literary titles are often revealed in the works they announce:

1. What is the prize in Shirley Jackson's story "The Lottery"?

2. Who is Charley in John Steinbeck's *Travels With Charley*?

3. Who is *The Catcher in the Rye* in J. D. Salinger's novel and why is he a catcher?

4. Why did George Orwell choose *Nineteen Eighty-Four* as the title and year of his novel?

5. Who is Algernon in Daniel Keyes's *Flowers for Algernon*?

6. In Joseph Heller's novel, what is *Catch-22*?

7. In T. S. Eliot's play *Murder in the Cathedral,* who was murdered?

8. What is *Mrs. Warren's Profession* in George Bernard Shaw's play by that name?

9. In what army is Shaw's *Major Barbara* a soldier?

10. What are the two cities in Charles Dickens's *A Tale of Two Cities*?

11. Why did Samuel Butler name his utopia *Erewhon*?

12. What is "The Windhover" in Gerard Manley Hopkins's poem?

13. In Nathaniel Hawthorne's *The Scarlet Letter,* what is the letter and what does it stand for?

14. What does *R.U.R.* stand for in Karel Čapek's play?

15. What does *wuthering* mean in Emily Brontë's *Wuthering Heights*?

16. In Alexandr Solzhenitsyn's *The Gulag Archipelago,* what do *gulag* and *archipelago* mean?

17. What is *Tono-Bungay* in the title of H. G. Wells's novel?

18. What is the speaker's modest proposal in "A Modest Proposal" by Jonathan Swift?

19. In Robert Browning's "The Pied Piper of Hamelin" and Gerard Manley Hopkins's "Pied Beauty," what does *pied* mean?

20. In William Golding's novel, who or what is the *Lord of the Flies*?

21. What is the jungle in Upton Sinclair's *The Jungle*?

22. In Stendhal's *The Charterhouse of Parma,* what is a charterhouse?

23. In Arthur Conan Doyle's "The Five Orange Pips," what are pips?

24. In *Out of the Silent Planet* and *Perelandra,* the next novel in the trilogy, what two planets is C. S. Lewis referring to in his titles?

25. What is the talisman in Walter Scott's *The Talisman*?

26. What is the lock in Alexander Pope's "The Rape of the Lock," and how was it "raped"?

27. What is the folly in Joseph Conrad's *Almayer's Folly*?

28. What is the name of the town in Thornton Wilder's play *Our Town*?

29. What is a scrivener in Herman Melville's story "Bartleby the Scrivener"?

30. What is the octopus in Frank Norris's *The Octopus*?

Mary Chase gave her tall tale a very short title, *Harvey*. Harvey isn't a person; he's a six-foot-one-inch make-believe rabbit seen only by his companion, the eccentric Elwood P. Dowd. The play was almost called *Daisy*, as Chase's original conception was of a four-foot-tall canary with that name.

Other titles do not reveal characters by name. Provide the name for each character referred to in each title:

31. Victor Hugo's *The Hunchback of Notre Dame*

32. James Fenimore Cooper's *The Last of the Mohicans*

33. Robert Bolt's *A Man For All Seasons*

34. Oliver Goldsmith's *The Vicar of Wakefield*

35. D. H. Lawrence's *Lady Chatterley's Lover*

36. Edward Everett Hale's *The Man Without a Country*

37. Alexandre Dumas's *The Three Musketeers*

38. Fyodor Dostoevsky's *The Brothers Karamazov*

39. Louisa May Alcott's *Little Women*

40. Richard Wright's *Native Son*

41. H. G. Wells's *The Invisible Man*

42. Ralph Ellison's *Invisible Man*

43. Oliver Wendell Holmes's *The Autocrat of the Breakfast-Table*

44. John Webster's *The White Devil*

45. Rudyard Kipling's *Stalky and Company*

46. Henry James's *The Portrait of a Lady*

47. Molière's *The Miser*

48. James Fenimore Cooper's *The Pathfinder*
49. George S. Kaufman and Moss Hart's *The Man Who Came to Dinner*
50. James Joyce's *A Portrait of the Artist as a Young Man*

ANSWERS

1. death by stoning 2. Steinbeck's pet poodle 3. Holden Caulfield, who hears the line in the Robert Burns song "If a body meet a body coming through the rye" as "If a body catch a body coming through the rye" 4. Orwell reversed the last two digits of 1948, the year in which he wrote much of the book, in order to show that within a single generation, democracy and freedom could be obliterated. 5. a laboratory rat

6. a military regulation that keeps the pilots in the story flying one suicidal mission after another 7. Thomas à Becket, Archbishop of Canterbury 8. prostitution 9. the Salvation Army 10. London and Paris

11. It's *Nowhere* spelled backward—almost. 12. a kestrel hawk, which hovers so gracefully above the wind 13. *A,* adultery 14. "Rossum's Universal Robots." In 1921 Čapek invented the word *robot,* from a Czech root meaning "to work," for his play. 15. making the sound of wind in the trees

16. *Gulag* is an acronym for the Russian words "Chief Administration of Collective Labor Camps." An archipelago is a cluster of islands, in this case an analogy to the network of prison sites spread throughout Russia. 17. a drug, a phony cure-all 18. that the children of poor people be sold as food for the tables of the rich 19. multicolored, blotched 20. a pig's head on a stick, the devil, or perhaps the darkness of the human heart

21. Chicago's meat-packing district 22. a monastery 23. seeds 24. Earth and Venus 25. an amulet with curative powers

26. a lock of hair of a real-life Miss Arabella Fermor, snipped off by one Robert Lord Petre 27. a house 28. Grover's Corner, New Hampshire 29. a professional copyist or scribe 30. the railroad

31. Quasimodo 32. Chingachgook and his son Uncas 33. Sir Thomas More 34. Dr. Charles Primrose 35. Oliver Mellors

36. Philip Nolan 37. Athos, Porthos, and Aramis 38. Dimitri, Ivan, Alyosha, and Smerdyakov 39. Meg, Jo, Beth, and Amy March 40. Bigger Thomas

41. Griffin 42. He is never named. 43. Oliver Wendell Holmes 44. Vittoria Corombona 45. Arthur Corkran

46. Isabel Archer 47. Harpagon 48. Natty Bumpo 49. Sheridan Whiteside 50. Stephen Dedalus

THE GAME IS THE NAME

■

One of the first things that each of us acquires when we enter this world is a name, and this name becomes the badge of our individuality. As poet James Russell Lowell wrote, "There is more force in names than most men dream of." Lewis Carroll recognized that force when he had Humpty Dumpty say to Alice, "My name means the shape I am—and a good handsome shape it is, too."

In their best-known form, the titles of many works of literature consist entirely of a character's name. Embedded in the two columns below are more than sixty titles. For most titles you will need to choose two names, one from each column, but a number of titles will use just a single word from either column. Also identify the author of each work:

Adam	Adams
Alice	Adverse
Anna	Andrews
Annabel	Arden
Anthony	Arrowsmith
Antigone	Babbitt
Barnaby	Bede
Benito	Brand

Billy   Budd
Camille   Burr
Christabel   Candide
Clarissa   Cereno
Cyrano   Cheevy
Daisy   Christie
Daniel   Chuzzlewit
Danny   Clinker
David   Copperfield
Elmer   Cory
Emma   Crusoe
Enoch   de Bergerac
Ethan   Deever
Eugene   Deronda
Eugénie   Din
Evangeline   Dodsworth
Gunga   Doone
Harvey   Dracula
Hedda   Esmond
Henry   Eyre
Hiawatha   Flanders
Humphrey   Frankenstein
Jane   Frome
Joseph   Gabler
Kim   Gantry
Lolita   Grandet
Lorna   Gray
Lucy   Herzog
Marjorie   Hudson
Martin   Ivanhoe
Miniver   Jones
Moll   Karenina
Nana   Lee
Nicholas   Marner
Oliver   Martin

Pamela	McTeague
Peter	Medea
Pierre	Miller
Pudd'nhead	Morningstar
Rebecca	Nickleby
Richard	Nostromo
Rip	Oblomov
Robinson	Onegin
Roderick	Ozymandias
Silas	Pan
Sula	Random
Tartuffe	Rudge
Tom	Shandy
Trilby	Twist
Tristram	Van Winkle
William	Wilson

The titles of many works of literature, like Brandon Thomas's *Charley's Aunt*, Richard Wright's *Uncle Tom's Children*, Alan Lightman's *Einstein's Dreams*, and Thomas Keneally's *Schindler's List* adhere to the *possessive name + noun* pattern. Without wiggling your Adam's apple over the prospect of opening a Pandora's box of Achilles' heels and Hobson's choices, fill in the thirty names that kick off each title and identify the author of each work:

1. _____'s Adventures in Wonderland
2. _____'s Baby
3. _____'s Body
4. _____'s Cabin
5. _____'s Castle
6. _____'s Choice
7. _____'s Complaint
8. _____'s Daughter
9. _____s End
10. _____'s Fan
11. _____'s Folly
12. _____'s Ghost
13. _____'s Gift
14. _____'s Last Case
15. _____'s Lives
16. _____'s Lover
17. _____'s Mines

18._____'s Needle   25._____'s Room
19._____'s Pendulum   26._____'s Schooldays
20._____'s People   27._____'s Travels
21._____'s Pilgrimage   28._____'s Wake
22._____'s Planet   29._____'s Way
23._____'s Profession   30._____'s Web
24._____'s Room

ANSWERS

Adam Bede, George Eliot; *Alice Adams,* Booth Tarkington; *Anna Karenina,* Leo Tolstoy; *Anna Christie,* Eugene O'Neill; "Annabel Lee," Edgar Allan Poe; *Anthony Adverse,* Hervey Allen; *Antigone,* Sophocles; *Arrowsmith,* Sinclair Lewis; *Babbitt,* Sinclair Lewis; *Barnaby Rudge,* Charles Dickens

"Benito Cereno," Herman Melville; *Billy Budd,* Herman Melville; *Brand,* Henrik Ibsen; *Burr,* Gore Vidal; *Camille,* Alexandre Dumas; "Christabel," Samuel Taylor Coleridge; *Candide,* Voltaire; *Clarissa,* Samuel Richardson; *Cyrano de Bergerac,* Edmond Rostand; *Daisy Miller,* Henry James

Daniel Deronda, George Eliot; *Daniel Martin,* John Fowles; "Danny Deever," Rudyard Kipling; *David Copperfield,* Charles Dickens; *Dodsworth,* Sinclair Lewis; *Dracula,* Bram Stoker; *Elmer Gantry,* Sinclair Lewis; *Emma,* Jane Austen; "Enoch Arden," Alfred, Lord Tennyson; "Ethan Brand," Nathaniel Hawthorne

Ethan Frome, Edith Wharton; *Eugene Onegin,* Alexander Pushkin; *Eugénie Grandet,* Honoré de Balzac; "Evangeline," Henry Wadsworth Longfellow; *Frankenstein,* Mary Wollstonecraft Shelley; "Gunga Din," Rudyard Kipling; *Harvey,* Mary Chase; *Hedda Gabler,* Henrik Ibsen; *Henry Esmond,* William Makepeace Thackeray; *Herzog,* Saul Bellow

"The Song of Hiawatha," Henry Wadsworth Longfellow; *Humphrey Clinker,* Tobias Smollett; *Ivanhoe,* Sir Walter Scott; *Jane Eyre,* Charlotte Brontë; *Joseph Andrews,* Henry Fielding; *Kim,* Rudyard Kipling; *Lolita,* Vladimir Nabokov; *Lorna Doone,*

Richard Doddridge Blackmore; "Lucy Gray," William Wordsworth; *Marjorie Morningstar*, Herman Wouk

Martin Chuzzlewit, Charles Dickens; *McTeague*, Frank Norris;
Medea, Euripides, Seneca; "Miniver Cheevy," Edwin Arlington
Robinson; *Moll Flanders*, Daniel Defoe; *Nana*, Émile Zola; *Nich-
olas Nickleby*, Charles Dickens; *Nostromo*, Joseph Conrad; *Oliver
Twist*, Charles Dickens; "Ozymandias," Percy Bysshe Shelley;
Oblomov, Ivan A. Goncharov

Pamela, Samuel Richardson; *Peter Pan*, James M. Barrie;
Pierre, Herman Melville; *Tragedy of Pudd'nhead Wilson*, Mark
Twain; *Rebecca*, Daphne Du Maurier; "Richard Cory," Edwin
Arlington Robinson; *Rip Van Winkle*, Washington Irving; *Rob-
inson Crusoe*, Daniel Defoe; *Roderick Hudson*, Henry James;
Roderick Random, Tobias Smollett

Silas Marner, George Eliot; *Sula*, Toni Morrison; *Tartuffe*,
Molière; *Tom Jones*, Henry Fielding; *Trilby*, George DuMaurier;
Tristram Shandy, Laurence Sterne; "William Wilson," Edgar
Allan Poe

1. *Alice*, Lewis Carroll 2. *Rosemary*, Ira Levin 3. *John Brown*,
Stephen Vincent Benét, 4. *Uncle Tom*, Harriet Beecher Stowe
5. *Lord Weary*, Robert Lowell 6. *Sophie*, William Styron
7. *Portnoy*, Philip Roth 8. *Rappaccini*, Nathaniel Hawthorne
9. *Howard*, E. M. Forster 10. *Lady Windermere*, Oscar Wilde

11. *Almayer*, Joseph Conrad 12. *Harlot*, Norman Mailer
13. *Humboldt*, Saul Bellow 14. *Trent*, Edmund Clerihew Bentley
15. *Dubin*, Bernard Malamud 16. *Lady Chatterley*, D. H. Lawrence. 17. *King Solomon*, H. Rider Haggard 18. *Gammer Gurton*,
William Stevenson, 19. *Foucault*, Umberto Eco 20. *Smiley*, John
Le Carré

21. *Childe Harold*, Lord Byron 22. *Mr. Sammler*, Saul Bellow
23. *Mrs. Warren*, George Bernard Shaw 24. *Giovanni*, James
Baldwin 25. *Jacob*, Virginia Woolf 26. *Tom Brown*, Thomas
Hughes 27. *Gulliver*, Jonathan Swift 28. *Finnegan*, James Joyce
29. *Swann*, Marcel Proust 30. *Charlotte*, E. B. White

THE MOTHER OF ALL TITLES

■

How many works have you read whose titles contain the preposition *of,* particularly the pattern *noun of a noun*? So many literary titles are cut from this fabricated cloth that the hundred examples that follow are but a small representation.

The *noun of a noun* pattern is so formulaic that we've chosen to present each title and author as a formula. Thus, "The F of the H of U, by E A P," and "The W of A F, by S B" reveal themselves as " 'The Fall of the House of Usher,' by Edgar Allan Poe," and *"The Way of All Flesh,* by Samuel Butler."

In taking this kind of test, most people solve fewer than half the problems on their first try, but they find that insights into additional answers come to them in sudden flashes when they return to the task a second or third time. The clues provided may be initially (get the pun?) confusing, but persevere and you will identify many, perhaps most, of the titles and authors:

1. The A of H F, by M T
2. The A of M J P, by E G
3. The A of M X, by A H
4. The A of T S, by M T
5. The A of the B-T, by O W H
6. The B of M C, by R J W
7. The B of R G, by O W

8. The B of the H-W, by
   E S V M
9. The B of the V, by T W
10. The C of A, by E A P
11. The C of an E O E, by
    T D Q
12. A C of D, by J K T
13. The C J F of C C, by
    M T
14. The C of E, by W S
15. The C of L 49, by T P
16. The C of M C, by A D
17. The C of N T, by W S
18. The C of the C B, by
    J A
19. The C of the W, by J L
20. D of a S, by A M
21. The D of a Y G, by A F
22. The D of the L, by N W
23. The D of W, by F F
24. E of E, by J S
25. The E of H K, by L R
26. An E of the P, by H I
27. F of F, by E J
28. The G of the M, by
    O H
29. The G of W, by J S
30. The H of B A, by F G L
31. H of D, by J C
32. The H of M, by E W
33. The H of N D, by V H
34. The H of the B, by
    A C D
35. The H of the M, by G G

36. The H of the S, by L C
37. The H of the S G, by
    N H
38. The I of B E, by O W
39. I of the K, by A, L T
40. The J of M, by C M
41. L of G, by W W
42. The L of S H, by W I
43. . . . and the L of the C,
    by H H S
44. L of the F, by W G
45. The L of the M, by
    J F C
46. The L of the W, by
    M R
47. The L S of J. A. P., by
    T S E
48. The M of A, by M R
49. The M of B, by R L S
50. The M of C, by T H
51. The M of E D, by C D
52. The M of the R D, by
    E A P
53. A M of the W, by C M
54. The M of V, by W S
55. N of the I, by T W
56. The N of the R, by U E
57. O D in the L of I D, by
    A S
58. The O of R F, by G M
59. The P of a L, by H J
60. P of the A, by P B
61. The P of D G, by O W
62. The P of M J B, by M S

63. The P of T, by P C

64. A P of the A as a Y M, by J J

65. The P of the W W, by J M S

66. The P P of the P C, by C D

67. The P of Z, by A H

68. The R B of C, by S C

69. The R of R C, by O H

70. The R of S L, by W D H

71. R of T P, by M P

72. The R of the A M, by S T C

73. The R of the L, by A P

74. The R of the N, by T H

75. The S H L of F M, by E H

76. The S L of W M, by J T

77. The S of B F, by W E B D

78. S of F, by K A P

79. The S of K, by E H

80. The S of M G S, by B G

81. The S of O T, by T W

82. S of S, by T M

83. The S of the L, by T H

84. T of A, by W S

85. T of C, by H M

86. A T of H, by S D

87. T of S, by E H

88. T of the A, by E R B

89. The T of the A M, by J P

90. T G of V, by W S

91. T of the D, by T H

92. The T of the S, by E B W (and H J and W S)

93. A T of T C, by C D

94. A T of the P, by E O

95. The V of H W, by S J

96. The V of W, by O G

97. The W of the H, by H W L

98. The W of the W, by H G W

99. The W of W, by H W

100. The W W of O, by L F B

Answers

1. *The Adventures of Huckleberry Finn,* by Mark Twain 2. *The Autobiography of Miss Jane Pittman,* by Ernest Gaines 3. *The Autobiography of Malcolm X,* by Alex Haley 4. *The Adventures of Tom Sawyer,* by Mark Twain 5. *The Autocrat of the Breakfast-Table,* by Oliver Wendell Holmes 6. *The Bridges of Madison County,* by Robert James Waller 7. "The Ballad of Reading Gaol," by Oscar Wilde 8. "The Ballad of the Harp-Weaver," by

Edna St. Vincent Millay 9. *The Bonfire of the Vanities*, by Tom Wolfe 10. "The Cask of Amontillado," by Edgar Allan Poe

11. *The Confessions of an English Opium Eater*, by Thomas de Quincey 12. *A Confederacy of Dunces*, by John Kennedy Toole 13. "The Celebrated Jumping Frog of Calaveras County," by Mark Twain 14. *The Comedy of Errors*, by William Shakespeare 15. *The Crying of Lot 49*, by Thomas Pynchon 16. *The Count of Monte Cristo*, by Alexandre Dumas 17. *The Confessions of Nat Turner*, by William Styron 18. *The Clan of the Cave Bear*, by Jean Auel 19. *The Call of the Wild*, by Jack London 20. *Death of a Salesman*, by Arthur Miller

21. *The Diary of a Young Girl*, by Anne Frank 22. *The Day of the Locust*, by Nathaniel West 23. *The Dogs of War*, by Frederic Forsyth 24. *East of Eden*, by John Steinbeck 25. *The Education of Hyman Kaplan*, by Leo Rosten 26. *An Enemy of the People*, by Henrik Ibsen 27. *Fear of Flying*, by Erica Jong 28. "The Gift of the Magi," by O. Henry 29. *The Grapes of Wrath*, by John Steinbeck 30. *The House of Bernarda Alba*, by Federico García Lorca

31. *Heart of Darkness*, by Joseph Conrad 32. *The House of Mirth*, by Edith Wharton 33. *The Hunchback of Notre Dame*, by Victor Hugo 34. "The Hound of the Baskervilles," by Arthur Conan Doyle 35. *The Heart of the Matter*, by Graham Greene 36. "The Hunting of the Snark," by Lewis Carroll 37. *The House of the Seven Gables*, by Nathaniel Hawthorne 38. *The Importance of Being Ernest*, by Oscar Wilde 39. "Idylls of the King," by Alfred, Lord Tennyson 40. *The Jew of Malta*, by Christopher Marlowe

41. *Leaves of Grass*, by Walt Whitman 42. "The Legend of Sleepy Hollow," by Washington Irving 43. *". . . and the ladies of the club,"* by Helen Hooven Santmeyer 44. *Lord of the Flies*, by William Golding 45. *The Last of the Mohicans*, by James Fenimore Cooper 46. *The Last of the Wine*, by Mary Renault 47. "The Love Song of J. Alfred Prufrock," by T. S. Eliot 48. *The Mask of Apollo*, by Mary Renault 49. *The Master of*

Ballantrae, by Robert Louis Stevenson 50. *The Mayor of Caster-bridge*, by Thomas Hardy

51. *The Mystery of Edwin Drood*, by Charles Dickens 52. "The Masque of the Red Death," by Edgar Allan Poe 53. *The Member of the Wedding*, by Carson McCullers 54. *The Merchant of Venice*, by William Shakespeare 55. *Night of the Iguana*, by Tennessee Williams 56. *The Name of the Rose*, by Umberto Eco 57. *One Day in the Life of Ivan Denisovich*, by Alexandr Solzhenitsyn 58. *The Ordeal of Richard Feverel*, by George Meredith 59. *The Portrait of a Lady*, by Henry James 60. *Planet of the Apes*, by Pierre Boulle

61. *The Picture of Dorian Gray*, by Oscar Wilde 62. *The Prime of Miss Jean Brodie*, by Muriel Spark 63. *The Prince of Tides*, by Pat Conroy 64. *A Portrait of the Artist as a Young Man*, by James Joyce 65. *The Playboy of the Western World*, by John Millington Synge 66. *The Posthumous Papers of the Pickwick Club*, by Charles Dickens 67. *The Prisoner of Zenda*, by Anthony Hope 68. *The Red Badge of Courage*, by Stephen Crane 69. "The Ransom of Red Chief," by O. Henry 70. *The Rise of Silas Lapham*, by William Dean Howells

71. *Remembrance of Things Past*, by Marcel Proust 72. *The Rime of the Ancient Mariner*, by Samuel Taylor Coleridge 73. "The Rape of the Lock," by Alexander Pope 74. *The Return of the Native*, by Thomas Hardy 75. "The Short Happy Life of Francis Macomber," by Ernest Hemingway 76. "The Secret Life of Walter Mitty," by James Thurber 77. *The Souls of Black Folks*, by W.E.B. Du Bois 78. *Ship of Fools*, by Katherine Anne Porter 79. "The Snows of Kilimanjaro," by Ernest Hemingway 80. *The Summer of My German Soldier*, by Bette Greene

81. *The Skin of Our Teeth*, by Thornton Wilder 82. *Song of Solomon*, by Toni Morrison 83. *The Silence of the Lambs*, by Thomas Harris 84. *Timon of Athens*, by William Shakespeare 85. *Tropic of Cancer* (and *Capricorn*), by Henry Miller 86. *A Taste of Honey*, by Shelagh Delaney 87. *Torrents of Spring*, by Ernest

Hemingway 88. *Tarzan of the Apes*, by Edgar Rice Burroughs 89. *The Teahouse of the August Moon*, by John Patrick 90. *Two Gentlemen of Verona*, by William Shakespeare

91. *Tess of the D'Urbervilles*, by Thomas Hardy 92. *The Trumpet of the Swan*, by E. B. White; *The Turn of the Screw*, by Henry James; *The Taming of the Shrew*, by William Shakespeare 93. *A Tale of Two Cities*, by Charles Dickens 94. *A Touch of the Poet*, by Eugene O'Neill 95. "The Vanity of Human Wishes," by Samuel Johnson 96. *The Vicar of Wakefield*, by Oliver Goldsmith 97. "The Wreck of the Hesperus," by Henry Wadsworth Longfellow 98. *The War of the Worlds*, by H. G. Wells 99. *The Winds of War*, by Herman Wouk 100. *The Wonderful Wizard of Oz*, by L. Frank Baum

THIS AND THAT

■

Many children have grown up hearing this ditty on the educational television series *The Electric Company*:

> *Conjunction, junction, what's your function?*
> *Hookin' up words and phrases and clauses.*

The conjunction *and* does indeed hook up two words in the titles of a number of works to make units that go together as naturally as love and marriage, home and hearth, peanut butter and jelly, and lox and bagel. Make the connection by joining each of the items from the first column with those in the second. Then identify each author.

And

Absalom	*Abel*
Advise	*Abelard*
The Agony	*Achitophel*
Androcles	*Ale*
Antony	*Anarchy*
Arms	*the Black*
Astrophel	*Brothers*
The Beautiful	*the Carpenter*
The Blue	*Cleopatra*
Bread	*Company*
Cabbages	*Consent*

Caesar	Cressida
Cakes	the Curmudgeon
The Cat	the Damned
The Cloister	Daniel Webster
Crime	the Dead
Culture	the Ecstasy
Decline	the English Language
The Devil	Fall
Eleanor	Franklin
Fathers	the Fury
Fire	the Glory
Franny	Goldmund
Gargantua	the Gray
Green Eggs	the Green Knight
Héloïse	Ham
Hero	the Hearth
Juno	Her Children
Kane	Ice
Man	Juliet
The Master	Kings
The Moon	Leander
Mother Courage	the Lion
Myra Breckinridge	Lovers
The Naked	the Man
Narcissus	Margarita
Of Mice	Men
Of Time	Myron
The Old Man	Pantagruel
The Owl	the Pauper
The Pit	the Paycock
The Plough	Peace
Politics	the Pendulum
The Power	Prejudice
Pride	Punishment
The Prince	the Pussy-Cat
The Red	Remembrance

Romeo	*the River*
Sense	*the Rock*
Sir Gawain	*the Sea*
Sons	*Sensibility*
The Sound	*Sixpence*
Stalky	*Sons*
Strangers	*the Stars*
Tea	*Stella*
Troilus	*Superman*
The Walrus	*Sympathy*
War	*Wine*
The Web	*Zooey*

ANSWERS

Absalom and Achitophel, John Dryden; *Advise and Consent*, Allen Drury; *The Agony and the Ecstasy*, Irving Stone; *Androcles and the Lion*, George Bernard Shaw; *Antony and Cleopatra*, William Shakespeare; *Arms and the Man*, George Bernard Shaw; *Astrophel and Stella*, Sir Philip Sidney; *The Beautiful and the Damned*, F. Scott Fitzgerald; *The Blue and the Gray*, Bruce Catton; *Bread and Wine*, Ignazio Silone

Cabbages and Kings, O. Henry; *Caesar and Cleopatra*, George Bernard Shaw; *Cakes and Ale*, W. Somerset Maugham; *The Cat and the Curmudgeon*, Cleveland Amory; *The Cloister and the Hearth*, Charles Reade; *Crime and Punishment*, Fyodor Dostoevsky; *Culture and Anarchy*, Matthew Arnold; *Decline and Fall*, Evelyn Waugh; "The Devil and Daniel Webster," Stephen Vincent Benét; *Eleanor and Franklin*, Joseph Lash

Fathers and Sons, Ivan Turgenev; "Fire and Ice," Robert Frost; *Franny and Zooey*, J. D. Salinger; *Gargantua and Pantagruel*, François Rabelais; *Green Eggs and Ham*, Dr. Seuss; *Héloise and Abelard*, George Moore; *Hero and Leander*, Christopher Marlowe; *Juno and the Paycock*, Sean O'Casey; *Kane and Abel*, Jeffrey Archer; *Man and Superman*, George Bernard Shaw

The Master and Margarita, Mikhail Bulgakov; *The Moon and*

Sixpence, W. Somerset Maugham; *Mother Courage and Her Children*, Bertold Brecht; *Myra Breckinridge and Myron*, Gore Vidal; *The Naked and the Dead*, Norman Mailer; *Narcissus and Goldmund*, Hermann Hesse; *Of Mice and Men*, John Steinbeck; *Of Time and the River*, Thomas Wolfe; *The Old Man and the Sea*, Ernest Hemingway; "The Owl and the Pussy-Cat," Edward Lear

"The Pit and the Pendulum," Edgar Allan Poe; *The Plough and the Stars*, Sean O'Casey; "Politics and the English Language," George Orwell; *The Power and the Glory*, Graham Greene; *Pride and Prejudice*, Jane Austen; *The Prince and the Pauper*, Mark Twain; *The Red and the Black*, Stendhal; *Romeo and Juliet*, William Shakespeare; *Sense and Sensibility*, Jane Austen; *Sir Gawain and the Green Knight*, the Pearl Poet

Sons and Lovers, D. H. Lawrence; *The Sound and the Fury*, William Faulkner; *Stalky and Company*, Rudyard Kipling; *Strangers and Brothers*, C. P. Snow; *Tea and Sympathy*, Robert Anderson; *Troilus and Cressida*, William Shakespeare (also Geoffrey Chaucer, *Troilus and Criseyde*); "The Walrus and the Carpenter," Lewis Carroll; *War and Remembrance*, Herman Wouk; *War and Peace*, Leo Tolstoy; *The Web and the Rock*, Thomas Wolfe

HEAVYWEIGHT TITLES

■

When writers create titles for their works, they draw their ideas from many sources—including the works of writers who have come before them. Take Ernest Hemingway as an example. He wrote a big novel about a man's personal commitment to a struggling people during the Spanish Civil War, and he sought a title that would express the interdependence of all men and women. Hemingway eventually found that title in a meditation composed by the early-seventeenth-century writer John Donne: "Any man's death diminishes me because I am involved in mankind; and therefore never send to know for whom the bell tolls; it tolls for thee."

Hemingway titled his novel *For Whom the Bell Tolls*.

Here are three dozen literary passages, each of which inspired the title of another famous literary work that came after. Identify the title inspired by each passage and the author of each work:

> 1. Mine eyes have seen the glory
>   Of the coming of the Lord;
>   He is tramping out the vintage
>   Where the grapes of wrath are stored.
>   —JULIA WARD HOWE, "BATTLE HYMN OF THE REPUBLIC"

2. What happens to a dream deferred?
   Does it dry up
   like a raisin in the sun?
   —Langston Hughes, "Harlem"

3. John Brown's body lies a-moldering in the grave,
   His soul is marching on.
   —Thomas Brigham Bishop, "John Brown's Body"

4. Humpty Dumpty sat on a wall:
   Humpty Dumpty had a great fall.
   All the King's horses and all the King's men
   Couldn't put Humpty Dumpty back together again.
   —Nursery Rhyme

5. Look homeward, Angel, now, and melt with ruth.
   And, O ye dolphins, waft the hapless youth.
   —John Milton, "Lycidas"

6. Far from the madding crowd's ignoble strife,
   Their sober wishes never learned to stray;
   Along the cool sequestered vale of life
   They kept the noiseless tenor of their way.
   —Thomas Gray, "Elegy Written in a Country
   Churchyard"

7. It Beareth the name of Vanity-Fair, because the
   town where 'tis kept, is lighter than Vanity.
   —John Bunyan, *The Pilgrim's Progress*

8. Away! away! for I will fly to thee,
   Not charioted by Bacchus and his pards,
   But on the viewless wings of Poesy,
   Though the dull brain perplexes and retards:
   Already with thee! tender is the night.
   —John Keats, "Ode to a Nightingale"

9. The best-laid schemes o' mice an' men,
   Gang aft a-gley,
   An' lea'e us naught but grief an' pain
   For promised joy!
   —ROBERT BURNS, "TO A MOUSE"

10. It is not a carol of joy or glee,
    But a prayer that he sends from his heart's deep
       core,
    But a plea, that upward to heaven he flings—
    I know why the caged bird sings!
    —PAUL LAURENCE DUNBAR, "SYMPATHY"

11. Go down, Moses, way down to Egypt land.
    Tell old Pharaoh: Let my people go.
    —AFRICAN AMERICAN SPIRITUAL

12. Of arms and the man I sing
    —VERGIL, *AENEID*

13. One flew east, one flew west,
    One flew over the cuckoo's nest.
    —NURSERY RHYME

14. "You and me, we've made a separate peace."
    —ERNEST HEMINGWAY, "A VERY SHORT STORY"

15. I have forgot much, Cynara! gone with the wind,
    Flung roses, roses riotously with the throng,
    Dancing, to put thy pale, lost lilies out of mind.
    —ERNEST DOWSON, "CYNARA"

16. Turning and turning in the widening gyre
    The falcon cannot hear the falconer;
    Things fall apart; the centre cannot hold;
    Mere anarchy is loosed upon the world.
    —WILLIAM BUTLER YEATS, "THE SECOND COMING"

17. Gentlemen-rankers out on the spree
    Damned from here to Eternity,
    God ha' mercy on such as we,
    Baa! Yah! Bah!
    —RUDYARD KIPLING, "GENTLEMEN-RANKERS"

18. Yet from those flames
    No Light, but rather darkness visible
    Served only to discover sights of woe,
    Regions of sorrow, doleful shades, where peace
    And rest can never dwell.
    —JOHN MILTON, PARADISE LOST

19. Yes, we'll rally round the flag, boys,
    We'll rally once again.
    Shouting the battle cry of Freedom.
    —GEORGE FREDERICK ROOT,
        "THE BATTLE CRY OF FREEDOM"

20. Seize the day, put no trust in the morrow!
    —HORACE, ODES, BOOK I, ODE XI

21. And a verse of a Lapland song
    Is haunting my memory still:
    "A boy's will is the wind's will,
    And the thoughts of youth are long, long
        thoughts."
    —HENRY WADSWORTH LONGFELLOW, "MY LOST YOUTH"

22. And what rough beast, its hour come round at last,
    Slouches towards Bethlehem to be born?
    —WILLIAM BUTLER YEATS, "THE SECOND COMING"

23. I will find out where she has gone
    And kiss her lips and take her hands;
    And walk among long dappled grass,
    And pluck till time and times are done
    The silver apples of the moon,
    The golden apples of the sun.
    —WILLIAM BUTLER YEATS,
    "THE SONG OF WANDERING AENGUS"

24. Well this side of Paradise! . . .
    There's little comfort in the wise.
    —RUPERT BROOKE, "TIARE TAHITI"

25. Oh, bang the drum slowly and play the fife lowly,
    And play the Dead March as you carry me along;
    Take me to the green valley, there lay the sod o'er
    me,
    For I'm a young cowboy, and I know I've done
    wrong.
    —ANON., "THE COWBOY'S LAMENT"

26. Though nothing can bring back the hour
    Of splendor in the grass, of glory in the flower.
    —WILLIAM WORDSWORTH,
    "ODE ON THE INTIMATIONS OF IMMORTALITY"

27. Between the dark and the daylight,
    When the night is beginning to lower,
    Comes a pause in the day's occupations
    That is known as the Children's Hour.
    —HENRY WADSWORTH LONGFELLOW,
    "THE CHILDREN'S HOUR"

28. His utmost power with adverse power opposed
    In dubious battle on the plains of heaven,
    And shook his throne.

    —JOHN MILTON, *PARADISE LOST*

29. I [Death] was astonished to see him in Baghdad,
    for I had an appointment with him tomorrow in
    Samarra.

    —W. SOMERSET MAUGHAM, *SHEPPY*

30. "The time has come," the Walrus said,
    "To talk of many things:
    Of shoes—and ships—and sealing wax—
    Of cabbages—and kings—
    And why the sea is boiling hot—
    And whether pigs have wings."

    —LEWIS CARROLL, "THE WALRUS AND THE CARPENTER"

31. When a true genius appears in the world, you
    may know him by this sign, that the dunces are
    all in confederacy against him.

    —JONATHAN SWIFT, "THOUGHTS ON VARIOUS SUBJECTS,
    MORAL AND DIVERTING"

32. Cast a cold eye
    On life, on death.
    Horseman, pass by!

    —WILLIAM BUTLER YEATS, "UNDER BEN BULBEN"

33. A Book of Verses underneath the Bough,
    A Jug of Wine, a Loaf of Bread—and thou
    Beside me singing in the Wilderness—
    Oh, Wilderness were Paradise enou!

    —EDWARD FITZGERALD, *RUBÁIYÁT OF OMAR KHAYYÁM*

34. Go tell it on the mountain,
    Over the hills and everywhere,
    Go tell it on the mountain
    That Jesus Christ is born.
                    —AFRICAN AMERICAN SPIRITUAL

35. Two roads diverged in a wood, and I—
    I took the one less traveled by,
    And that has made all the difference.
                    —ROBERT FROST, "THE ROAD NOT TAKEN"

36. I could give all to Time except—except
    What I myself have held. But why declare
    The things forbidden that while the Customs slept
    I have crossed to Safety with? For I am There
    And what I would not part with I have kept.
                    —ROBERT FROST, "I COULD GIVE ALL TO TIME"

ANSWERS

1. *The Grapes of Wrath*, John Steinbeck 2. *A Raisin in the Sun*, Lorraine Hansberry 3. *John Brown's Body*, Stephen Vincent Benét 4. *All the King's Men*, Robert Penn Warren 5. *Look Homeward, Angel*, Thomas Wolfe 6. *Far from the Madding Crowd*, Thomas Hardy 7. *Vanity Fair*, William Makepeace Thackeray 8. *Tender Is the Night*, F. Scott Fitzgerald 9. *Of Mice and Men*, John Steinbeck 10. *I Know Why the Caged Bird Sings*, Maya Angelou

11. *Go Down, Moses*, William Faulkner 12. *Arms and the Man*, George Bernard Shaw 13. *One Flew Over the Cuckoo's Nest*, Ken Kesey 14. *A Separate Peace*, John Knowles 15. *Gone with the Wind*, Margaret Mitchell 16. *Things Fall Apart*, Chinua Achebe

17. *From Here to Eternity*, James Jones 18. *Darkness Visible*, William Styron 19. *Rally Round the Flag, Boys!*, Max Shulman 20. *Seize the Day*, Saul Bellow

21. *A Boy's Will*, Robert Frost 22. *Slouching Towards Bethlehem*, Joan Didion 23. *The Golden Apples of the Sun*, Ray Bradbury (also *The Golden Apples*, Eudora Welty; *Golden Apples*, Marjorie Kinnan Rawlings) 24. *This Side of Paradise*, F. Scott Fitzgerald 25. *Bang the Drum Slowly . . .* , Mark Harris 26. *Splendor in the Grass*, William Inge 27. *The Children's Hour*, Lillian Hellman 28. *In Dubious Battle*, John Steinbeck 29. *An Appointment in Samarra*, John O'Hara 30. *Cabbages and Kings*, O. Henry

31. *A Confederacy of Dunces*, John Kennedy Toole 32. *Horseman, Pass By!*, Larry McMurtry and *Cast a Cold Eye*, Mary McCarthy 33. *Ah, Wilderness!*, Eugene O'Neill 34. *Go Tell It on the Mountain*, James Baldwin 35. *The Road Less Traveled*, M. Scott Peck 36. *Crossing to Safety*, Wallace Stegner

OR WHAT YOU WILL

∎

Many lovers of literature have read or know about *Clarissa*, but few of them are aware that the full title of Samuel Richardson's novel is *Clarissa, or the History of a Young Lady Comprehending the Most Important Matters of Private Life*. Match the subtitles that follow with their main titles and name each author:

1. *The Autobiography of a Horse*
2. *The Contemplative Man's Recreation*
3. *The Fox*
4. *"From Recollections of Early Childhood"*
5. *The Imposter*
6. *Life Among the Lowly*
7. *Life in the Woods*
8. *The Mistakes of a Night*
9. *The Modern Prometheus*
10. *The Moor of Venice*
11. *The New Pilgrim's Progress*
12. *A Novel Without a Hero*
13. *Optimism*

"Bartleby the Scrivener"
Ben-Hur

Black Beauty
Candide

The Compleat Angler
"The Deacon's Masterpiece"
"Ecclesiastes"
Frankenstein
The Hobbitt
The Innocents Abroad
Maggie: A Girl of the Streets
Moby-Dick
"Ode on the Intimations of Immortality"

14. *The Parish Boy's Progress*	*Oliver Twist*
15. *A Peep at Polynesian Life*	*Othello*
16. "The Preacher"	*She Stoops to Conquer*
17. *A Pure Woman*	*Silas Marner*
18. "A Story of Wall Street"	*Tartuffe*
19. *A Story of New York*	*Tess of the D'Urbervilles*
20. *A Tale of the Christ*	*Twelfth Night*
21. *There and Back Again*	*Typee*
22. *The Weaver of Raveloe*	*Uncle Tom's Cabin*
23. *The Whale*	*Vanity Fair*
24. *What You Will*	*Volpone*
25. "The Wonderful 'One-Hoss Shay' "	*Walden*

ANSWERS

1. *Black Beauty*, Anna Sewell 2. *The Compleat Angler*, Isaak Walton 3. *Volpone*, Ben Jonson 4. "Ode on the Intimations of Immortality," William Wordsworth 5. *Tartuffe*, Molière

6. *Uncle Tom's Cabin*, Harriet Beecher Stowe 7. *Walden*, Henry David Thoreau 8. *She Stoops to Conquer*, Oliver Goldsmith 9. *Frankenstein*, Mary Wollstonecraft Shelley 10. *Othello*, William Shakespeare

11. *The Innocents Abroad*, Mark Twain 12. *Vanity Fair*, William Makepeace Thackeray 13. *Candide*, Voltaire 14. *Oliver Twist*, Charles Dickens 15. *Typee*, Herman Melville

16. "Ecclesiastes" 17. *Tess of the D'Urbervilles*, Thomas Hardy 18. "Bartleby the Scrivener," Herman Melville 19. *Maggie: A Girl of the Streets*, Stephen Crane 20. *Ben-Hur*, Lew Wallace

21. *The Hobbitt*, J.R.R. Tolkien 22. *Silas Marner*, George Eliot 23. *Moby-Dick*, Herman Melville 24. *Twelfth Night*, William Shakespeare 25. "The Deacon's Masterpiece," Oliver Wendell Holmes

ROYALTIES

■

The first royalties were paid to kings by the commoners for the right to operate royal properties and use royal resources. Nowadays authors, like the monarchs of old, are paid royalties by publishers for the right to use their ideas and creations for profit. It's a shame that few authors actually do live like kings.

Who wrote these works with titles peopled by noble personages?:

1. *The Emperor Jones*
2. *The Emperor's New Clothes*
3. *Oedipus Rex*
4. *A Connecticut Yankee in King Arthur's Court*
5. *Idylls of the King*
6. *The Once and Future King*
7. *The King Must Die*
8. *King Lear*
9. *The Return of the King*
10. *King Solomon's Mines*
11. *Cabbages and Kings*
12. *King Rat*
13. *The Man Who Would Be King*
14. *The Mambo Kings Play Songs of Love*
15. *The Faerie Queene*
16. *The King Who was King*

17. *Queen Mab*
18. *The Beet Queen*
19. *The African Queen*
20. *Queen*
21. *Mary, Queen of Scots*
22. *Queen of the Damned*
23. *The Prince*
24. *The Little Prince*
25. *The Prince and the Pauper*
26. *The Prince of Tides*
27. *Princess Daisy*
28. "My Last Duchess"
29. *The Count of Monte Cristo*
30. *Lord of the Flies*
31. *Lord Jim*
32. *Lord Weary's Castle*
33. *Little Lord Fauntleroy*
34. *Lady Windermere's Fan*
35. *Lady Chatterley's Lover*

ANSWERS

1. Eugene O'Neill 2. Hans Christian Andersen 3. Sophocles
4. Mark Twain 5. Alfred, Lord Tennyson 6. T. H. White
7. Mary Renault 8. William Shakespeare 9. J.R.R. Tolkien
10. H. Rider Haggard

11. O. Henry 12. James Clavell 13. Rudyard Kipling
14. Oscar Hijuelos 15. Edmund Spenser 16. H. G. Wells
17. Percy Bysshe Shelley 18. Louise Erdrich 19. C. S. Forester
20. Alex Haley

21. Antonia Fraser 22. Anne Rice 23. Niccolò Machiavelli
24. Antoine de Saint-Exupéry 25. Mark Twain 26. Pat Conroy
27. Judith Krantz 28. Robert Browning 29. Alexandre Dumas
30. William Golding

31. Joseph Conrad 32. Robert Lowell 33. Frances Burnett
34. Oscar Wilde 35. D. H. Lawrence

Works

TRY THESE FOR OPENERS

■

Isaac Asimov tells the story of the author whose agent told him his books weren't selling because there wasn't enough sex in them. "Not enough sex?" the writer shouted. "Look, right here on the first page of my latest novel the courtesan dashes out of the room stark naked and runs out into the street with the hero hotly pursuing her just as naked and in an explicitly described state of sexual arousal."

"Yes, yes," said the agent, "but look how *far down* the first page!"

"Write dramatic, button-holing leads to your stories," James Thurber's editor commanded during his early days as a newspaper reporter. In response, Thurber turned in a murder story that began: "Dead. That's what the man was when they found him with a knife in his back at 4 P.M. in front of Riley's Saloon at the corner of 52nd and 12th Streets."

Some beginnings are so effective and well known that readers can look at them and identify the literary works that they lead off. Using the lists of titles and authors that follow, identify the novel or short story started by each sentence and the author of each work:

1. Call me Ishmael.
2. Nothing to be done.

3. It is a truth universally acknowledged, that a single man in possession of a good fortune, must be in want of a wife.

4. It was a bright cold day in April, and the clocks were striking thirteen.

5. Brrrrrriiiiiiiiiiiiiiiiiinng!

6. Whether I shall turn out to be the hero of my own life, or whether that station will be held by anybody else, these pages must show.

7. It was Wang Lung's marriage day.

8. It was love at first sight.

9. To the red country and part of the gray country of Oklahoma, the last rains came gently, and they did not cut the scarred earth.

10. She was one of those pretty, charming ladies, born, as if through an error of destiny, into a family of clerks.

11. As Gregor Samsa awoke one morning from uneasy dreams, he found himself transformed into a giant insect.

12. Buck did not read the newspapers or he would have known that trouble was brewing, not alone for himself, but for every tide-water dog, strong of muscle and with warm, long hair, from Puget Sound to San Diego.

13. The boy with fair hair lowered himself down the last few feet of rock and began to pick his way toward the lagoon.

14. A green and yellow parrot, which hung in a cage outside the door, kept repeating over and over: *"Allez vous-en! Allez vous-en!"*

15. When he was nearly thirteen, my brother Jem got his arm badly broken at the elbow.

16. A squat grey building of only thirty-four stories.

17. It was a dark and stormy night . . .

18. They're out there.

19. "Christmas won't be Christmas without any presents," grumbled Jo, lying on the rug.

20. What can you say about a twenty-five-year-old girl who died?

21. He was an old man who fished alone in a skiff in the Gulf Stream and he had gone eighty-four days now without taking a fish.

22. When Mrs. Frederick C. Little's second son arrived, everybody noticed that he was not much bigger than a mouse.

23. A throng of bearded men, in sad-colored garments and gray, steeple-crowned hats, intermixed with women, some wearing hoods, and others bareheaded, was assembled in front of a wooden edifice, the door of which was heavily timbered with oak, and studded with iron spikes.

24. One thing was certain, that the *white* kitten had had nothing to do with it—it was the black kitten's fault entirely.

25. Once upon a time and a very good time it was there was a moocow coming down along the road and this moocow that was coming down along the road met a nicens little boy named baby tuckoo . . .

Titles	*Authors*
The Awakening	Louisa May Alcott
Brave New World	Jane Austen
The Call of the Wild	Samuel Beckett
Catch-22	Pearl Buck
David Copperfield	Edward Bulwer-Lytton
The Good Earth	Lewis Carroll
The Grapes of Wrath	Kate Chopin
Little Women	Charles Dickens
Lord of the Flies	William Golding
Love Story	Nathaniel Hawthorne
"The Metamorphosis"	Joseph Heller
Moby-Dick	Ernest Hemingway
Native Son	Aldous Huxley
"The Necklace"	James Joyce
Nineteen Eighty-Four	Franz Kafka
The Old Man and the Sea	Ken Kesey
One Flew Over the Cuckoo's Nest	Harper Lee

Paul Clifford   Jack London

A Portrait of the Artist As a Young   Guy de Maupassant
   Man

Pride and Prejudice   Herman Melville

The Scarlet Letter   George Orwell

Stuart Little   Erich Segal

Through the Looking-Glass   John Steinbeck

To Kill a Mockingbird   E. B. White

Waiting for Godot   Richard Wright

ANSWERS

1. *Moby-Dick,* Herman Melville 2. *Waiting for Godot,* Samuel Beckett 3. *Pride and Prejudice,* Jane Austen 4. *Nineteen Eighty-Four,* George Orwell 5. *Native Son,* Richard Wright 6. *David Copperfield,* Charles Dickens 7. *The Good Earth,* Pearl Buck 8. *Catch-22,* Joseph Heller 9. *The Grapes of Wrath,* John Steinbeck 10. "The Necklace," Guy de Maupassant

11. "The Metamorphosis," Franz Kafka 12. *The Call of the Wild,* Jack London 13. *Lord of the Flies,* William Golding 14. *The Awakening,* Kate Chopin 15. *To Kill a Mockingbird,* Harper Lee 16. *Brave New World,* Aldous Huxley 17. *Paul Clifford,* Edward Bulwer-Lytton 18. *One Flew Over the Cuckoo's Nest,* Ken Kesey 19. *Little Women,* Louisa May Alcott 20. *Love Story,* Erich Segal

21. *The Old Man and the Sea,* Ernest Hemingway 22. *Stuart Little,* E. B. White 23. *The Scarlet Letter,* Nathaniel Hawthorne 24. *Through the Looking-Glass,* Lewis Carroll 25. *A Portrait of the Artist As a Young Man,* James Joyce

UNREAL ESTATE

■

He wrote under the pseudonyms Schuyler Stanton, Floyd Akers, and Edith Van Dyne, but he is best known as L. Frank Baum. In 1900, he sat down to write a children's book about a girl named Dorothy, who was swept away to a fantastic land inhabited by munchkins and witches and a scarecrow, a tin man, and a lion.

The fairy tale began as a bedtime story for Baum's children and their friends and soon spilled over into several evening sessions. During one of the tellings, Baum was asked the name of the strange place to which Dorothy was swept away. Glancing about the room, Baum's eyes fell upon the drawers of a filing cabinet labeled "A–N" and "O–Z."

Noting that the letters on the second label spelled out the *ahs* uttered by his rapt listeners, Baum named his fantastic land Oz. Ever since, *The Wonderful Wizard of Oz* has lived in the hearts of children—and grown-ups. Translated into at least thirty languages, it is the best-selling juvenile book of all time.

For many lovers of literature, places that exist only between the covers of books are as vivid as places that actually exist on gas station maps. If you are one of those people for whom Oz is as real as Oslo, Camelot as real as Camden, and Wonderland as real as Disneyland, this quiz is for you.

Match each literary locale listed in the left-hand column with the name of its creator listed in the right-hand column:

1. Barchester	Sherwood Anderson
2. Baskerville Hall	Piers Anthony
3. Belle Reve	Aristophanes
4. Bensalem	Margaret Atwood
5. Bleak House	Jane Austen
6. Brewster Place	Francis Bacon
7. Brideshead	James Barrie
8. Cloud Cuckoo Land	L. Frank Baum
9. Darkover	Marion Zimmer Bradley
10. Devon School	Charlotte Brontë
11. Dune	Emily Brontë
12. East Egg	John Bunyan
13. East Lynne	Samuel Butler
14. Egdon Heath	Lewis Carroll
15. The Emerald City	Miguel de Cervantes
16. Erewhon	Samuel Taylor Coleridge
17. The Forest of Arden	Charles Dickens
18. Gilead	Arthur Conan Doyle
19. Gopher Prairie	Daphne du Maurier
20. La Mancha	George Eliot
21. Land of the Lotus-Eaters	William Faulkner
22. Lilliput	F. Scott Fitzgerald
23. Looking-Glass House	Kenneth Grahame
24. Lowood	Thomas Hardy
25. Manderley	Frank Herbert
26. Middle Earth	James Hilton
27. Middlemarch	Homer
28. Narnia	Stephen King
29. Never-Never-Land	John Knowles
30. Northanger Abbey	C. S. Lewis
31. Oceania	Sinclair Lewis
32. Pandemonium	A. A. Milne
33. Pencey Prep	John Milton
34. Pooh Corner	Thomas More
35. The Republic	Gloria Naylor

36. Salem's Lot	George Orwell
37. Serendip	Plato
38. Shangri-La	Edwin Arlington Robinson
39. The Slough of Despond	J. D. Salinger
40. Starkville	Sir Walter Scott
41. Toad Hall	William Shakespeare
42. Thrushcross Grange	B. F. Skinner
43. Tilbury Town	Jonathan Swift
44. Utopia	J.R.R. Tolkien
45. Walden Two	Anthony Trollope
46. Waverley Honour	Horace Walpole
47. Winesburg	Evelyn Waugh
48. Xanadu	Edith Wharton
49. Xanth	Tennessee Williams
50. Yoknapatawpha County	Mrs. Henry Wood

ANSWERS

1. Anthony Trollope 2. Arthur Conan Doyle 3. Tennessee Williams 4. Francis Bacon 5. Charles Dickens 6. Gloria Naylor 7. Evelyn Waugh 8. Aristophanes 9. Marion Zimmer Bradley 10. John Knowles

11. Frank Herbert 12. F. Scott Fitzgerald 13. Mrs. Henry Wood 14. Thomas Hardy 15. L. Frank Baum 16. Samuel Butler 17. William Shakespeare 18. Margaret Atwood 19. Sinclair Lewis 20. Miguel de Cervantes

21. Homer 22. Jonathan Swift 23. Lewis Carroll 24. Charlotte Brontë 25. Daphne du Maurier 26. J.R.R. Tolkien 27. George Eliot 28. C. S. Lewis 29. James Barrie 30. Jane Austen

31. George Orwell 32. John Milton 33. J. D. Salinger 34. A. A. Milne 35. Plato 36. Stephen King 37. Horace Walpole 38. James Hilton 39. John Bunyan 40. Edith Wharton

41. Kenneth Grahame 42. Emily Brontë 43. Edwin Arlington Robinson 44. Thomas More 45. B. F. Skinner 46. Sir Walter Scott 47. Sherwood Anderson 48. Samuel Taylor Coleridge 49. Piers Anthony 50. William Faulkner

WORLD SERIES

■

Earlier in this book we saw that two or more authors working together can be better than one. The same holds true for works of literature, which may be bonded together in a series.

A series of novels is a collection that traces through several books the adventures and development of a single character or group of characters. The first type we see in the Nancy Drew and Tom Swift books and the second in those novels by William Faulkner that chronicle the decline of the Sartoris, Benbow, and McCaslin families and the rise of the Snopeses.

The following books make up which trilogies? Identify their authors:

1. *Agamemnon, Choëphoroe (The Libation Bearers), The Eumenides*

2. *Inferno, Purgatorio, Paradiso*

3. *The 42nd Parallel, 1919, The Big Money*

4. *The Fellowship of the Ring, The Two Towers, Return of the King*

5. *The Good Earth, Sons, A House Divided*

Who wrote these series?:

6. *Leather-Stocking Tales*

7. *Foundation Trilogy*

8. *Studs Lonigan: A Trilogy*

9. *The Alexandria Quartet*

10. *The Forsyte Saga*

11. *Chronicles of Barsetshire*
12. *The Xanth Series*
13. *Earth's Children*
14. *The Deptford Trilogy*
15. *Joseph and His Brothers*
16. *Tales of My Landlord*
17. *Strangers and Brothers*
18. *Les Rougon-Macquart*
19. *The Clayhanger Trilogy*
20. *The Rosy Crucifixion*

Poems, too, can gain momentum when they are clustered and read together. Following Petrarch's and Shakespeare's examples, a number of poets have written series of sonnets that are linked in their exploring various aspects of a relationship between lovers. Who wrote the following sonnet sequences?:

21. *Amoretti*
22. *Sonnets From the Portuguese*
23. *Astrophel and Stella*
24. *The House of Life*
25. *Two Lives*

ANSWERS

1. The *Oresteia*, Aeschylus 2. *The Divine Comedy*, Dante 3. *U.S.A.*, John Dos Passos 4. *Lord of the Rings*, J.R.R. Tolkien 5. *The House of Earth*, Pearl Buck 6. James Fenimore Cooper 7. Isaac Asimov 8. James T. Farrell 9. Lawrence Durrell 10. John Galsworthy

11. Anthony Trollope 12. Piers Anthony 13. Jean Auel 14. Robertson Davies 15. Thomas Mann 16. Sir Walter Scott 17. C. P. Snow 18. Émile Zola 19. Arnold Bennett 20. Henry Miller

21. Edmund Spenser 22. Elizabeth Barrett Browning 23. Sir Philip Sidney 24. Dante Gabriel Rossetti 25. William Ellery Leonard

STILL HOT OFF THE PRESS

■

Ezra Pound once defined literature as "news that stays news." The plots spun out by many classic works of literature are as contemporary as today's headlines, especially as they are screamed in the tabloids. Just think what the *National Enquirer* and *Star* would do with the stories told in famous books if they had actually happened. What literary plots are reflected in the following lurid headlines? Name the author who wrote each grisly tale:

1. KING KILLS HIS FATHER, THEN MARRIES
   WOMAN OLD ENOUGH TO BE HIS MOTHER—
   AND SHE IS!

2. CHICAGO CHAUFFEUR SMOTHERS BOSS'S DAUGHTER,
   THEN CUTS HER UP AND STUFFS HER IN FURNACE

3. GARAGE OWNER STALKS AFFLUENT BUSINESSMAN,
   THEN SHOTGUNS HIM IN HIS SWIMMING POOL

4. DOCTOR'S WIFE AND LOCAL MINISTER EXPOSED
   FOR CONCEIVING ILLEGITIMATE DAUGHTER

5. COLLAR FACTORY EMPLOYEE CONVICTED
   OF DROWNING PREGNANT GIRLFRIEND

6. VERONA TEENAGERS COMMIT DOUBLE SUICIDE;
   FAMILIES VOW TO END CLAN VENDETTA

7. STUDENT CONFESSES TO AXE MURDER
   OF LOCAL PAWNBROKER AND ASSISTANT

8. MADWOMAN LONG IMPRISONED IN ATTIC
   SETS HOUSE ON FIRE, THEN LEAPS TO DEATH

9. FORMER SCHOOLTEACHER,
   FOUND TO HAVE BEEN PROSTITUTE,
   COMMITTED TO INSANE ASYLUM

10. GOV'T. OFFICIAL'S WIFE,
    BEARING COUNT'S CHILD,
    FLINGS SELF UNDER TRAIN

11. GHOSTS OF FORMER SERVANTS
    HAUNT GOVERNESS, CHILDREN

12. SKELETON OF WINE TASTER DISCOVERED
    BEHIND BRICK WALL IN MANSION CELLAR

13. RETARDED ITINERANT FARMWORKER
    CRUSHES BOSS'S DAUGHTER-IN-LAW;
    THEN MERCY-KILLED BY BEST FRIEND

14. MAYOR FOUND TO HAVE AUCTIONED
    OFF WIFE AND DAUGHTER TO SAILOR

15. STEPMOTHER STRANGLES HER BABY
    TO PROVE LOVE FOR HER STEPSON;
    BOTH GIVE THEMSELVES UP

16. SUFFERING FROM
      MULTIPLE PERSONALITY DISORDER,
   PROMINENT LONDON DOCTOR
      FINALLY KILLS SELVES

17. MAROONED ON CORAL ISLAND,
   BRITISH PREPPIES KILL EACH OTHER

18. WOMAN RAISED IN CONVENT,
   CAUGHT IN WEB OF SEX
   AND DEBT, TAKES ARSENIC

19. PRINCE ACQUITTED OF KILLING MOTHER
   IN REVENGE FOR MURDER OF HIS FATHER

20. BRIDGE IN PERU COLLAPSES;
   FIVE PLUNGE TO THEIR DEATHS

21. DENTIST WHO BLUDGEONED WIFE FOUND DEAD
   IN DEATH VALLEY HANDCUFFED TO PURSUER

22. MOTHER PLOTS MERCY KILLING OF SON
   AFFLICTED WITH A SOCIAL DISEASE

23. WOMAN KNITS WHOLE WARDROBES
   DURING PUBLIC EXECUTIONS

24. LORD OF MANOR FRIGHTENED TO DEATH
   BY PHOSPHORESCENT GIANT DOG

25. MASS. ADULTERERS SURVIVE DUAL SUICIDE PACT;
   ATTEMPTED TO RAM THEIR SLED INTO TREE

ANSWERS

1. *Oedipus Rex*, Sophocles 2. *Native Son*, Richard Wright 3. *The Great Gatsby*, F. Scott Fitzgerald 4. *The Scarlet Letter*, Nathaniel Hawthorne 5. *An American Tragedy*, Theodore Dreiser 6. *Romeo and Juliet*, William Shakespeare 7. *Crime and Punishment*, Fyodor Dostoevsky 8. *Jane Eyre*, Charlotte Brontë 9. *A Streetcar Named Desire*, Tennessee Williams 10. *Anna Karenina*, Leo Tolstoy

11. *The Turn of the Screw*, Henry James 12. "The Cask of Amontillado," Edgar Allan Poe 13. *Of Mice and Men*, John Steinbeck 14. *The Mayor of Casterbridge*, Thomas Hardy 15. *Desire Under the Elms*, Eugene O'Neill 16. *The Strange Case of Dr. Jekyll and Mr. Hyde*, Robert Louis Stevenson 17. *Lord of the Flies*, William Golding 18. *Madame Bovary*, Gustave Flaubert 19. *Eumenides* (in *Oresteia*), Aeschylus 20. *The Bridge of San Luis Rey*, Thornton Wilder

21. *McTeague*, Frank Norris 22. *Ghosts*, Henrik Ibsen 23. *A Tale of Two Cities*, Charles Dickens 24. "The Hound of the Baskervilles," Arthur Conan Doyle 25. *Ethan Frome*, Edith Wharton

NOTABLE, QUOTABLE POETRY

■

"There's no money in poetry," quoth the poet laureate Robert Graves, "but there's also no poetry in money." While it is true that rhyme doesn't pay, poets gain a foothold on eternity through their poems, which for some people is even better than money. What follows are some of the most memorable and enduring lines in the mighty line of English poetry. Identify the sources of the following quotations by title and author:

1. Whan that Aprill with his shoures soote
   The droghte of March hath perced to the roote

2. Shall I compare thee to a summer's day?
   Thou art more lovely and more temperate

3. Death be not proud

4. 'Twas brillig, and the slithy toves
   Did gyre and gimble in the wabe:
   All mimsy were the borogoves,
   And the mome raths outgrabe.

5. Drink to me only with thine eyes,
   And I will pledge with mine

6. Listen, my children, and you shall hear
   Of the midnight ride of Paul Revere,
   On the eighteenth of April, in seventy-five;
   Hardly a man is now alive
   Who remembers that famous day and year.

7. The outlook wasn't brilliant for the Mudville
        nine that day;
   The score stood four to two, with but one inning
        more to play.

8. Gather ye rosebuds while ye may,
   Old Time is still a-flying

9. Once upon a midnight dreary, while I pondered,
        weak and weary,
   Over many a quaint and curious volume of
        forgotten lore,—

10. I could not love thee, Dear, so much,
    Loved I not Honor more.

11. But at my back I always hear
    Time's wingèd chariot hurrying near

12. They also serve who only stand and wait

13. Know then thyself, presume not God to scan;
    The proper study of mankind is man

14. Should auld acquaintance be forgot,
    And never brought to min'?

Should auld acquaintance be forgot,
And days o' auld lang syne?

15. Tiger! Tiger! burning bright
In the forests of the night.
What immortal hand or eye
Could frame thy fearful symmetry?

16. Water, water, everywhere,
Nor any drop to drink

17. Hope springs eternal in the human breast

18. A thing of beauty is a joy forever

19. If winter comes, can spring be far behind?

20. Beauty is truth, truth beauty

21. A Book of Verses underneath the Bough,
A Jug of Wine, a Loaf of Bread—and Thou

22. God's in his heaven—
All's right with the world.

23. How do I love thee? Let me count the ways

24. A little learning is a dangerous thing.

25. Do not go gentle into that good night. . . .
Rage, rage against the dying of the light.

26. To the glory that was Greece,
And the grandeur that was Rome

27. By the shores of Gitche Gumee,
    By the shining Big-Sea-Water

28. Behind him lay the gray Azores,
    Behind the Gates of Hercules;
    Before him not the ghost of shores,
    Before him only shoreless seas.

29. Build thee more stately mansions, O my soul

30. O Captain! my Captain! our fearful trip is done,
    The ship has weathered every rack, the prize we
        sought is won.

31. Because I could not stop for Death,
    He kindly stopped for me—

32. This is the way the world ends
    Not with a bang but a whimper.

33. The fog comes
    on little cat feet.

34. The woods are lovely, dark and deep.
    But I have promises to keep

35. Out of the night that covers me,
    Black as the Pit from pole to pole,
    I thank whatever gods may be
    For my unconquerable soul.

36. I must down to the seas again, to the lonely sea
    and the sky,
    And all I ask is a tall ship and a star to steer her by.

37. And we are here as on a darkling plain
    Swept with confused alarms of struggle and flight,
    Where ignorant armies clash by night.

38. A poem should not mean
    But be.

39. Theirs not to make reply,
    Theirs not to reason why,
    Theirs but to do and die;
    Into the valley of Death
    Rode the six hundred.

40. An' the Gobble-uns 'at gits you
        Ef you
           Don't
              Watch
                Out!

ANSWERS

1. *The Canterbury Tales,* Geoffrey Chaucer 2. Sonnet XVIII,
William Shakespeare 3. "Death Be Not Proud," John Donne
4. "Jabberwocky," Lewis Carroll 5. "Song: To Celia," Ben
Jonson 6. "Paul Revere's Ride," Henry Wadsworth Longfellow
7. "Casey at the Bat," Ernest Lawrence Thayer 8. "To the
Virgins, to Make Much of Time," Robert Herrick 9. "The
Raven," Edgar Allan Poe 10. "To Lucasta, Going to the Wars,"
Richard Lovelace
    11. "To His Coy Mistress," Andrew Marvell 12. "On His
Blindness," John Milton 13. "An Essay on Man," Alexander

Pope 14. "Auld Lang Syne," Robert Burns 15. "The Tiger,"
William Blake 16. "The Rime of the Ancient Mariner," Samuel
Taylor Coleridge 17. "Essay on Man," Alexander Pope
18. *Endymion,* John Keats 19. "Ode to the West Wind," Percy
Bysshe Shelley 20. "Ode on a Grecian Urn," John Keats

21. *The Rubáiyát of Omar Khayyám,* Edward FitzGerald
22. *Pippa Passes,* Robert Browning 23. from *Sonnets from the
Portuguese,* Elizabeth Barrett Browning 24. "Essay on Criti-
cism," Alexander Pope 25. "Do Not Go Gentle into That Good
Night," Dylan Thomas 26. "To Helen," Edgar Allan Poe
27. "The Song of Hiawatha," Henry Wadsworth Longfellow
28. "Columbus," Joaquin Miller 29. "The Chambered Nauti-
lus," Oliver Wendell Holmes 30. "O Captain! My Captain!,"
Walt Whitman

31. "Because I could not stop for Death," Emily Dickinson
32. "The Hollow Men," T. S. Eliot 33. "Fog," Carl Sandburg
34. "Stopping by Woods on a Snowy Evening," Robert Frost
35. "Invictus," William Ernest Henley 36. "Sea-Fever," John
Masefield 37. "Dover Beach," Matthew Arnold 38. "Ars Po-
etica," Archibald MacLeish 39. "The Charge of the Light Brigade," Alfred, Lord Tennyson 40. "Little Orphant Annie,"
James Whitcomb Riley

WAR GAME

∎

"Like me to write you a little essay on The Importance of Subject?" wrote Ernest Hemingway to F. Scott Fitzgerald. "Well the reason you are so sore you missed the war is because war is the best subject of all. It groups the maximum of material and speeds up the action and brings out all sorts of stuff that normally you have to wait a lifetime to get."

Fitzgerald was commissioned a second lieutenant in the U.S. Army Infantry in 1917, but never served abroad, while Hemingway was an American Red Cross ambulance driver in Italy during World War I. A number of other writers have had firsthand experience with that "best subject of all." Ambrose Bierce enlisted twice in the Ninth Indiana Infantry and fought in a great many Civil War skirmishes and battles including Philippi and Shiloh. In 1867 he was promoted to major in recognition of his heroism and distinguished service, and later wrote some twenty-five short stories about his war experiences, among them "An Occurrence at Owl Creek Bridge" and "Chickamauga." In 1862 and 1863 Walt Whitman served as a copyist in the army paymaster's office and spent his afternoons nursing the wounded in nearby military hospitals. He recorded his experiences and emotions in *Drum Taps*.

By far the best-known novel about the American Civil War is Stephen Crane's *The Red Badge of Courage*. So vividly realistic is Crane's account of Henry Fleming's discoveries of war and his own manhood that many readers believe the author must have fought in the war. In fact, a number of Civil War veterans swore up and down that Crane had fought next to them on the battlefield. But Crane never participated in the War Between the States, one convincing proof being the fact that he was not born until 1871.

The following works are grouped according to the wars they describe. Name the war and the author of each work:

1. *April Morning; Johnny Tremaine; Drums Along the Mohawk; The Spy*
2. *John Brown's Body; Andersonville; Gone with the Wind*
3. *A Farewell to Arms; All Quiet on the Western Front; The Enormous Room;* "Dulce Et Decorum Est"
4. *The Green Berets; Dog Soldiers; Going After Cacciato*
5. *Catch-22; A Bell for Adano; The Naked and the Dead; Slaughterhouse-Five*
6. *For Whom the Bell Tolls*
7. "The Charge of the Light Brigade"
8. "Old Ironsides"; *Captain Caution*
9. *A Tale of Two Cities*
10. *War and Peace*
11. *The Bridges at Toko-Ri*
12. *The Last of the Mohicans; Montcalm and Wolfe*
13. *Henry V*
14. *The Talisman*
15. *The Song of Roland*
16. *Lysistrata; The Last of the Wine*
17. *Iliad; Troilus and Criseyde*
18. *Ten Days That Shook the World*
19. *Man's Fate*
20. *The Biglow Papers*, Series 1

ANSWERS

1. American Revolutionary War: Howard Fast, Esther Forbes, Walter D. Edmonds, James Fenimore Cooper 2. American Civil War: Stephen Vincent Benét, MacKinlay Kantor, Margaret Mitchell 3. World War I: Ernest Hemingway, Erich Maria Remarque, e.e. cummings, Wilfred Owen 4. Vietnam War: Robin Moore, Robert Stone, Tim O'Brien 5. World War II: Joseph Heller, John Hersey, Norman Mailer, Kurt Vonnegut 6. Spanish Civil War: Ernest Hemingway 7. Crimean War: Alfred, Lord Tennyson 8. War of 1812: Oliver Wendell Holmes, Kenneth Roberts 9. French Revolution: Charles Dickens 10. Napoleonic Wars: Leo Tolstoy

11. Korean War: James Michener 12. French and Indian War: James Fenimore Cooper, Francis Parkman 13. The Hundred Years' War: William Shakespeare 14. The Crusades: Sir Walter Scott 15. battles of Charlemagne: anonymous 16. Peloponnesian Wars: Aristophanes, Mary Renault 17. Trojan War: Homer, Geoffrey Chaucer (also William Shakespeare) 18. Russian Revolution: John Reed 19. Chinese Revolution: André Malraux 20. The Mexican War: James Russell Lowell

LANGUAGE THROWS
THE BOOK AT US

■

When people misuse words in an illiterate but humorous manner, we call the result a *malapropism*. The word echoes the name
of Mrs. Malaprop (from the French *mal à propos*, "not appropriate"), a character who first strode the stage in 1775 in Richard
Sheridan's comedy *The Rivals*. Mrs. Malaprop was an "old
weather-beaten she dragon" who took special pride in her use
of the King's English but who unfailingly mangled big words all
the same: "Sure, if I reprehend anything in this world it is the
use of my oracular tongue, and a nice derangement of epitaphs!"
She meant, of course, that if she comprehended anything, it was
a nice arrangement of epithets.

In his epic poem *Paradise Lost*, John Milton invented Pandemonium—literally "a place for all the demons"—as the name
of the home for Satan and his devilish friends. Because the devils
were noisy, the meaning of *pandemonium*, now lowercased, has
been broadened to mean "uproar and tumult."

A number of words like *malapropism* and *pandemonium* have
been literally and literarily born at the tip of a pen, for our
language bestows a special kind of life upon people and places
that have existed only in books. Fictional creations though they

may be, many of these literary creations have assumed a vitality and longevity that pulse just as powerfully as their flesh-and-blood counterparts. The words that derive from these imaginary names can achieve such wide application that they are no longer written with capital letters.

Using the following descriptions, identify the common words that have sprung from the fertile imaginations of our novelists, playwrights, and poets. Also identify the original names of the characters or works whence they sprung:

1. The hero of a novel by Miguel de Cervantes engaged himself in endless knightly quests, rescuing damsels he deemed to be in distress and fighting monsters by tilting against windmills. An adjective formed from his name now describes people who are idealistic and chivalrous to an extravagant degree.

2. The name of a blustering giant in Edmund Spenser's Renaissance epic, *The Faerie Queene,* has become a word for a loud-mouthed boaster who is notably short on performance.

3. Another big-talking giant lumbers through the pages of a novel by François Rabelais. This giant king was so huge that it took 17,913 cows to provide him with milk and 1,100 hides to make him a pair of shoes. Today an adjective form of his name denotes anything of a colossal scale.

4. In 1516 Sir Thomas More wrote a book about an ideal state. As a name for both the novel and the place, More coined a name from the Greek word parts *ou,* "no," *topos,* "place," and *-ia,* "state of being." The resulting word has come to designate any ideal society.

5. The imagination of Charles Dickens teemed with colorful characters who so embodied particular traits in human nature that their names have come to stand for those qualities. Thus, a fawning toady is often called a *Uriah Heep* and a tyrannical teacher a *Gradgrind. Micawberish* has become a synonym for "habitually hopeful" and *Pecksniffery* a noun for religious hypocrisy.

These name words have retained their capital letters, but one that is rapidly evolving into lowercase began life as a character in *A Christmas Carol*. Even though old Ebenezer's heart turned from stone to gold at the end of the story, we still use his name to describe a mean and miserly person.

A special kind of populist literature is the comic strip, and the cartoon characters and stories that we encounter in our newspapers and on our movie screens have exerted a considerable influence on our language. The first successful American comic strip was "Yellow Kid" in Joseph Pulitzer's *New York World*. The feature made its debut in 1895 and was printed in attention-grabbing yellow ink. As early as 1898 the phrase "yellow journalism" was applied to sensational stories of crime and corruption that ran in papers like the *World*.

Identify the comic strip words that have not drawn their last breath, as well as their pen-and-ink sources:

6. In 1928 Walt Disney gave the world Mickey, an all-American rodent who performed heroic deeds and squeaked his undying love for Minnie. Soon after World War II, European markets were flooded with wristwatches bearing this character's likeness. Because these watches were generally cheap affairs, subject to chronic and chronometric main-spring breakdowns, people started associating anything shoddy or trivial with this character's name.

7. The name of H. T. Webster's wimpy comic strip character has become synonymous with a meek, unassertive man.

8. Speaking of *wimpy*, linguists disagree about the origins of this vogue adjective. Some contend that *wimpy* is a form of the verb *whimper*. Others trace the word back to a pot-bellied fellow who devoured hamburgers in E. C. Segar's "Popeye" comic strip, which began in the late 1920s.

9. Another rotund comic strip character, this one created by

David Low, inspired us to apply metaphorically the name of a floating airship to people endowed with an abundance of adipose tissue.

10. "On the_____," meaning "not operating properly," may have started with one of the earliest comic strips, "The Katzenjammer Kids." Typically, the two hyperactive German boys caused all sorts of trouble for the Captain and other adults in the story.

ANSWERS

1. quixotic—Don Quixote 2. braggadocio—Braggadocio 3. gargantuan—Gargantua 4. utopia—*Utopia* 5. scrooge—Scrooge 6. mickey mouse—Mickey Mouse 7. milquetoast—Caspar Milquetoast 8. wimpy—J. Wellington Wimpy 9. blimp—Colonel Blimp 10. fritz—Fritz

BOOKS IN THE NEWS

■

Back in 1986, the citizens of New England were electrified by the gallant charge that the Boston Red Sox made into the World Series. An editorial in one New England newspaper crowed, "The titans of the East have done it: The Red Sox and the Mets will meet in the baseball World Series, and all is right with the world."

The Red Sox won the first two games of the Series in alien Shea Stadium and then lost the next two games at home, at which point appeared the headline "There Was No Joy in Fenway." The team salvaged the next game and four times were one strike away from their first world championship in sixty-eight years. But somehow they managed to snatch defeat from the jaws of victory and lost both the sixth and seventh games, prompting this headline: "Another Winter of Discontent for New England."

The editorial statement springs from Robert Browning's *Pippa Passes*:

> *The lark's on the wing;*
> *The snail's on the thorn;*
> *God's in his heaven—*
> *All's right with the world!*

The first headline paraphrases the ballad "Casey at the Bat," written by Ernest Lawrence Thayer:

> Oh! somewhere in this favored land
>   The sun is shining bright,
> The band is playing somewhere,
>   And somewhere hearts are light;
> And somewhere men are laughing,
>   And somewhere children shout,
> But there is no joy in Mudville—
>   Mighty Casey has struck out.

The second headline, written after the Red Sox collectively struck out the Series, echoes the opening line of Shakespeare's *Richard III*:

> Now is the winter of our discontent
> Made glorious summer by this son of York.

Our lives are considerably enriched when we are able to spot such sources: allusions allow us to experience an idea on two levels at once by linking what we are reading or hearing with what we have read or heard in the past. By enhancing the present through associations with experiences that glow through time, allusions open doors of perception.

The richest source of present-day allusions is literature. Each quotation that follows appeared in a newspaper or magazine, and each alludes to a literary source. As specifically as you can, identify each literary source:

1. The Kaufmans say that the medical community forces them into a Catch-22 situation. If they make significant progress with a child, doctors question whether the child was autistic. If no change occurs, doctors reject them as failures.

2. The basic problem with *A Second Chance* has little to do with the authors' data, presentation, or optimistic vision of a

New Hampshire energy future without Seabrook. It is that Seabrook exists, rather like Bertha in the attic in *Jane Eyre*.

3. For many Americans April is indeed the cruelest month because it contains April 15, the deadline for filing tax returns to the Internal Revenue Service.

4. There's no question for whom the bell tolls in Chile. It tolls for General Augusto Pinochet and for the dictatorship that has run Chile since 1973.

5. Do You Dare to Eat a Peach? (title of a magazine article on contaminated fruit)

6. He stoppeth one of three. (from a story about a hapless New Jersey Devils hockey goalie)

7. Hockey superstar Wayne Gretzky is often referred to as "The Great Gretzky."

8. *CBS News Sunday Morning* comes into our living rooms on little cat's feet.

9. For the next six months, Walesa guided that union across lines that no one dared dream possible in Eastern Europe. Visions of independence danced in Polish heads.

10. Here's an old bone he threw out at the 1988 Republican National Convention: "A kinder, gentler nation," a great-sounding notion. Sometimes, after all, George Bush had a great notion.

11. Shuttling from one capital to another, [Secretary of State James] Baker is operating on the Panglossian premise that the world's statesmen can eventually work something out.

12. A Budget of Dreams Deferred. (headline for a story about the New York City budget)

13. That the Giants still can get into the playoffs as a wild-card entry is damnation, which now is damnation by faint praise.

14. It was the worst of times for Faust; it was the best of times for two other coaches who have been the targets of numerous critics—Alabama's Ray Perkins and Tennessee's Johnny Majors.

15. Crashes, explosions and other disasters are, like the shadows on the wall of Plato's cave, only the shadow of the news.

16. The crabmeat in most seafood salads never spent any time in a pair of ragged claws scuttling across the floors of silent seas. It was made in a blender.

17. Once again he fell short, leaving Wimbledon without the championship that has become an obsession. Ahab in this tennis version of Moby Dick, Ivan Lendl will find solace in the belief that he is getting closer to his goal, that eventually, all the hard work and sweat will be rewarded.

18. She gave the last full measure of devotion to excellence in education. We will prove our resolve that she shall not have died in vain when we have lifted New Hampshire to the top in its respect for good schools. (from a column about the fallen astronaut Christa McAuliffe)

19. Aging Stars Rage Against the Dying of the Light. (headline of a story on older athletes playing baseball for the California Angels)

20. Life in Azerbaijan is nasty, brutish, and short.

ANSWERS

1. The title of Joseph Heller's *Catch-22* refers to a military regulation that keeps pilots flying insanely suicidal missions. "Catch-22," now meaning "a problematic situation whose very nature denies any rational solution," has become the most frequently employed allusion in all of American literature. 2. The Seabrook nuclear power plant in New Hampshire, like the mad Bertha Mason in Charlotte Brontë's *Jane Eyre,* simply will not disappear. Ultimately, Bertha sets fire to the house in which she is imprisoned and is consumed in the conflagration. 3. As the opening of T. S. Eliot's poem *The Waste Land* tells us, "April is the cruelest month." 4. The title of Ernest Hemingway's novel *For Whom the Bell Tolls* hearkens back to a sermon by John Donne: "Any man's death diminishes me because I am involved in mankind; and therefore never send to know for whom the bell tolls; it tolls for thee." 5. In T. S. Eliot's "The Love Song of J. Alfred Prufrock," the wimpy speaker endlessly worries about whether he should "dare to eat a peach." After all, a peach has all that juice in it and a hard pit at its center.

6. A brilliant reference to Samuel Taylor Coleridge's "The Rime of the Ancient Mariner." The Mariner "stoppeth one of three" to tell his story of crime and punishment over and over again. 7. Gretzky's epithet is an allusion to F. Scott Fitzgerald's glittering hero, the Great Gatsby. 8. Carl Sandburg's "Fog" opens with "The fog comes / on little cat feet." 9. From Clement Moore's "The Night Before Christmas": "While visions of sugar-plums danced in their heads." 10. From Ken Kesey's *Sometimes a Great Notion,* itself an allusion to the song "Goodnight Irene": "Sometimes I live in the country, / Sometimes I live in town; / Sometimes I take a great notion / To jump into the river and drown."

11. In *Candide,* Voltaire satirizes Dr. Pangloss ("all tongue") for his eternally optimistic view of life. His constant refrain is "All is for the best in this best of all possible worlds."

12. Langston Hughes's "Harlem" begins: "What happens to a dream deferred? / Does it dry up / like a raisin in the sun?" 13. In Alexander Pope's "Epistle to Dr. Arbuthnot" appears the paradox "Damn with faint praise, assent with civil leer, / And without sneering, teach the rest to sneer." 14. Among the best known of novelistic openers is the one from Charles Dickens's *A Tale of Two Cities:* "It was the best of times, it was the worst of times, it was the age of wisdom, it was the age of foolishness. . . ." 15. A learned reference to the allegory that Plato presents in Book VII of *The Republic* to show that most people apprehend but a shadow of reality.

16. A clever twist of the couplet from T. S. Eliot's "The Love Song of J. Alfred Prufrock": "I should have been a pair of ragged claws / Scuttling across the floors of silent seas." 17. In Herman Melville's *Moby-Dick*, Captain Ahab obsessively pursues the white whale, which becomes more that a great fish and instead is a symbol of our impossible efforts to attain great goals and to make sense of the universe. As Ahab chased Moby Dick to no avail, Ivan Lendl never won a Wimbledon tournament. 18. From Abraham Lincoln's Gettysburg Address: "It is rather for us to be here dedicated to the great task remaining before us—that from these honored dead we take increased devotion to the cause for which they gave the last full measure of devotion; that we here highly resolve that these dead shall not have died in vain." 19. In "Do Not Go Gentle into That Good Night," poet Dylan Thomas urges his father, "Do not go gentle into that good night, / Old age should burn and rave at close of day; / Rage, rage against the dying of the light." 20. An allusion to Thomas Hobbes's assertion in *Leviathan* that human life is "nasty, brutish, and short."

LITERARY MISCONCEPTIONS

∎

"I hate soccer," wrote William F. Reed in a July 1990 issue of *Sports Illustrated,* "and I'm tired of being made to feel guilty about it. So there. I feel better now. Call me an ugly American, but please don't try to sell me the World Cup."

In a *Newsday* piece published six months later, Timothy Phelps observed, "[Saddam Hussein's message] has been bolstered by his willingness to defy not only the ugly Americans, whose culture and political power threaten Arab moral values and independence as much as the Persians ever did . . ."

What's wrong with the statements above? Look again at Reed's and Phelps's use of the epithets "ugly American" and "ugly Americans." Both writers employ the phrase to signify a citizen of the United States who has little appreciation for things foreign. Indeed, "ugly American" has become such a catchphrase in the English language that it is enshrined in *Merriam-Webster's Collegiate Dictionary, Tenth Edition* (1993): "an American in a foreign country whose behavior is offensive to the people of that country."

Merriam-Webster traces "Ugly American" (capitalized in that dictionary) to *The Ugly American* (1958), a collection of stories written by William J. Lederer and Eugene L. Burdick.

Reed's, Phelps's, and the dictionary's sense of the epithet

constitutes one of the most universal of literary misconceptions in the English-speaking world—that an "ugly American" is one who exhibits uncomely behavior. In the title story of Lederer and Burdick's collection, the ugly American is a man named Homer Atkins, an engineer sent to Vietnam to work in heavy construction. The grease-spattered Atkins is indeed ugly in appearance (hence the Ugly American), but he is also culturally sensitive, hardheaded, and honest about his task: "Of course you've got good people out there in the boondocks, good hardworking people who are plenty savvy. But they don't want what you want yet. It takes time for that. That's why I recommend in my report that you start small, with little things. And then after you lick them, go on to bigger things. Hell, we could build dams and roads for you, but you don't have the skill or capacity or need for them now."

Ultimately, Atkins is assigned to the boondocks of Sarkhan, where, with the help of an "ugly Sarkhanese" named Jeepo, he invents and implements a man-powered water pump to lift the water from one terraced rice paddy to another in the Sarkhanese villages. So the original ugly American, with his integrity and pragmatic effectiveness, is anything but ugly in the sense of that term today.

Poor Homer Atkins, a literary allusion who has become an illusion. Of all the characters in *The Ugly American,* he is the most aware of the cultural context and needs of people in Southeast Asia. If he were real, he might sue for defamation of literary character.

Here are questions about other expressions, characters, and titles that were born from the tip of a pen and that are often misapplied in everyday parlance. Compare your answers with those that follow the questions:

1. What is "the lion's share"?
2. Who was Frankenstein?
3. Would you like to have "the Midas touch"?

4. What is the "immaculate conception," and where in the Bible do we find the phrase?

5. In a title such as *Apologia pro Vita Sua,* by Cardinal Newman, what does *Apologia* mean?

6. In the expression "The hand that rocks the cradle rules the world," who is the cradle-rocker?

7. Does the saying "A rolling stone gathers no moss" support or criticize the wandering, knockabout life?

8. To what does the smithy refer in the famous opening lines of Henry Wadsworth Longfellow's "The Village Smithy"?:

> *Under a spreading chestnut tree*
> *The village smithy stands.*

9. In Shakespeare's line "O Romeo, Romeo! wherefore art thou Romeo?" what does *wherefore* mean?

10. In *Hamlet,* the melancholy prince talks about "a custom more honored in the breach than the observance," one of the myriad of Shakespearean phrases that lives today. What exactly does "more honored in the breach than the observance" mean?

Answers

1. In the original Aesop's fable, the Lion threatens the Fox, Jackal, and Wolf and ends up eating the entire stag. Literally, and literarily, "the lion's share" means the whole shebang, ball of wax, and shootin' match, not just a portion larger than anyone else's.

2. Frankenstein refers to the mad doctor (actually the young medical student) in Mary Wollstonecraft Shelley's classic horror novel, not the Boris Karloff character. Old Zipperneck is properly alluded to as Frankenstein's monster. Therefore, the cliché "creating a Frankenstein" makes no sense.

3. Most people would, because most people interpret the Midas touch to mean success in matters financial, the ability to make everything one touches turn to gold. In Greek mythology, King Midas was a monarch in Asia Minor who was granted the wish of the golden touch. The problem was that everything, including his food and drink, turned to gold. When even his beloved daughter became transmuted, he begged to have the gift withdrawn and had to bathe in the Pactolus River to remove what was a curse, not a blessing.

4. It is a misconception to believe that "the immaculate conception" refers to the birth of Jesus Christ. Rather, it designates the doctrine that Mary was born without any taint of original sin. This doctrine was not declared by the Roman Catholic Church to be an article of faith until 1854, when Pope Pius IX issued the Bull *Ineffabilis Deus*. Hence, the phrase "immaculate conception" does not appear in the Bible.

5. *Apologia* issues from a Late Latin word that means "a justification or defense," not "a statement of regret." *Apology* ultimately descends from the Greek *apologein*, "to tell fully," and in his *Apologia* Newman recounts his spiritual development.

6. As indicated by the title of the popular motion picture *The Hand That Rocks the Cradle*, almost everybody thinks that the hand is attached to mothers. But the cradle-rocker is God, as is evident from the original context of the line in "The Hand That Rules the World," by the nineteenth-century American poet Ross Wallace:

> They say that man is mighty,
>   He governs land and sea.
> He wields a mighty sceptre
>   O'er lesser powers that be;
> But a mightier power and stronger
>   Man from his throne has hurled,
> For the hand that rocks the cradle
>   Is the hand that rules the world.

7. Thomas Tusser's *A Hundred Points of Good Husbandrie* (1557) makes it clear that people who are always on the move and don't settle down will never become prosperous:

> *The stone that is rolling can gather no moss,*
> *For master and servant oft changing is loss.*

8. A smithy is a blacksmith's shop, not a blacksmith. The ironworker is a smith, as the next two lines of Longfellow's poem indicate:

> *The smith, a mighty man is he,*
> *With large and sinewy hands.*

9. A careful examination of Shakespeare's use of *wherefore*—"Wherefore rejoice? / What conquest brings he home?" (*Julius Caesar*); "But wherefore could I not pronounce 'Amen'?" (*Macbeth*)—reveals that *wherefore* means "why," not "where." Further proof is the redundant cliché "the whys and wherefores." Those who recite the line from *Romeo and Juliet* should be sure to emphasize the name *Romeo,* rather than the word *art.*

10. Nowadays we use "More honored in the breach than the observance" to mean that something is more often broken than observed. Hamlet's original remark, however, referred to the Danes' penchant for boozing. He meant that the more honorable course was to breach the custom—to stay cold sober rather than get stinking drunk.

ALL'S WELL THAT ENDS WELL

■

"L-d, said my mother, what is all this story about?—A COCK and a BULL, said Yorick—And one of the best kind I ever heard" is the sprightly ending of Laurence Sterne's *Tristram Shandy*. Cock and bull stories are so called because ancient fables were filled with birds and animals walking and talking and acting like people.

The problem with stories, cock and bull or not, is that they must be wound up. In that process, some go dead, while others conclude memorably. "Great is the art of the beginning, but greater the art is of ending," wrote Thomas Fuller in *Gnomologia*. From the list that follows, select the titles and name the authors of the literary works, quoted below, that end well:

1. But I reckon I got to light out for the Territory ahead of the rest because Aunt Sally she's going to adopt me and sivilize me and I can't stand it. I been there before.

2. After all, tomorrow is another day.

3. So we beat on, boats against the current, borne back ceaselessly into the past.

4. Villains! I shrieked, dissemble no more! I admit the deed!—tear up the planks!—here! here!—it is the beating of his hideous heart!

5. They endured.

6. Don't ever tell anybody anything. If you do, you start missing everybody.

7. It is a far, far better thing that I do, than I have ever done; it is a far, far better rest that I go to, than I have ever known.

8. Who knows but that, on lower frequencies, I speak for you.

9. So I awoke, and behold, it was a dream.

10. I lingered round them, under that benign sky: watched the moths fluttering among the heath and harebells: listened to the soft wind breathing through the grass; and wondered how any one could ever imagine unquiet slumbers for the sleepers in that quiet earth.

11. That might be the subject of a new story—but our present story is ended.

12. Vale.

13. There were three thousand six hundred and fifty-three days like this in his sentence, from reveille to lights out. The three extra ones were because of the leap years.

14. There is more day to dawn. The sun is but a morning star.

15. Nowadays the world is lit by lightning! Blow out your candles, Laura—and so goodbye . . .

Titles	*Authors*
The Adventures of Huckleberry Finn	Emily Brontë
The Catcher in the Rye	John Bunyan
Crime and Punishment	Miguel de Cervantes
Don Quixote	Charles Dickens
The Glass Menagerie	Fyodor Dostoevsky
The Great Gatsby	Ralph Ellison
Gone with the Wind	F. Scott Fitzgerald
Invisible Man	William Faulkner
One Day in the Life of Ivan Denisovich	Margaret Mitchell
Pilgrim's Progress	Edgar Allan Poe
The Sound and the Fury	J. D. Salinger
A Tale of Two Cities	Alexandr Solzhenitsyn

"The Tell-Tale Heart"	Henry David Thoreau
Walden	Mark Twain
Wuthering Heights	Tennessee Williams

Answers

1. *The Adventures of Huckleberry Finn*, Mark Twain 2. *Gone with the Wind*, Margaret Mitchell 3. *The Great Gatsby*, F. Scott Fitzgerald 4. "The Tell-Tale Heart," Edgar Allan Poe 5. *The Sound and the Fury*, William Faulkner 6. *The Catcher in the Rye*, J. D. Salinger 7. *A Tale of Two Cities*, Charles Dickens 8. *Invisible Man*, Ralph Ellison 9. Part One of *Pilgrim's Progress*, John Bunyan 10. *Wuthering Heights*, Emily Brontë

11. *Crime and Punishment*, Fyodor Dostoevsky 12. *Don Quixote*, Miguel de Cervantes 13. *One Day in the Life of Ivan Denisovich*, Alexandr Solzhenitsyn 14. *Walden*, Henry David Thoreau 15. *The Glass Menagerie*, Tennessee Williams

The Bible

IN THEIR OWN WORDS

■

The word *bible* derives from the Greek *biblia,* which means "books." Indeed, the Bible is a whole library of books that contain many different kinds of literature—history, narrative, short stories, poetry, philosophy, riddles, fables, allegories, letters, and drama. Many parts of the Bible are highly dramatic because they show in detail the sweep of grand events as experienced by a vivid and diverse cast of persons.

As their hopes and fears, ambitions and tragedies, and laughter and sorrows unfold in the Bible, many of these men and women have become so familiar to so many readers that they have become archetypal. Thus, a large man is a Goliath, an old man a Methuselah, a wise man a Solomon, a traitorous man a Judas, an evil woman a Jezebel, a doer of good deeds a good Samaritan, a patient man a Job, a skeptical man a doubting Thomas, a mighty hunter a Nimrod, and a strong man a Samson (while his luggage is Samsonite).

Many of these people reveal themselves through what they say. From their own words, identify these biblical personages:

1. "Am I my brother's keeper?"
2. "For whither thou goest I will go; and where thou lodgest, I will lodge; thy people shall be my people, and thy God my God."

3. "Let my people go."

4. "O my son Absalom, my son, my son Absalom! would God I had died for thee, O Absalom, my son, my son!"

5. "My God, my God, why hast thou forsaken me?"

6. "O Lord God, remember me, I pray thee, and strengthen me, I pray thee, only this once, O God, that I may be at once avenged of the Philistines for my two eyes."

7. "Naked came I out of my mother's womb, and naked shall I return thither: the Lord gave, and the Lord hath taken away; blessed be the name of the Lord."

8. "Take me up, and cast me forth into the sea; so shall the sea be calm unto you: for I know that for my sake this great tempest is upon you."

9. "My God hath sent his angel, and hath shut the lions' mouths, that they have not hurt me."

10. "Thou art the man. Thus saith the Lord God of Israel, I anointed thee king over Israel, and I delivered thee out of the hand of Saul."

11. "Divide the living child in two, and give half to the one, and half to the other."

12. "Why have ye conspired against me, thou and the son of Jesse?"

13. "After I am waxed old shall I have pleasure, my lord being old also?"

14. "Behold the fire and the wood: but where is the lamb for a burnt offering?"

15. "The serpent beguiled me, and I did eat."

16. "Feed me, I pray thee, with that same red pottage; for I am faint."

17. "Hereby ye shall know that the living God is among you, and that he will without fail drive out from before you the Canaanites."

18. "Am I not a Philistine, and ye servants to Saul? Choose you a man for you, and let him come down to me. If he be able to fight with me, and to kill me, then will we be your servants."

19. "Take ye him, and crucify him: for I find no fault in him."

20. "If it please the king, and if I have found favor in his sight, and the thing seem right before the king, and I be pleasing in his eyes, let it be written to reverse the letters devised by Haman the son of Hammedatha the Agagite, which he wrote to destroy the Jews which are in all the king's provinces."

21. "I am Esau thy firstborn; I have done according as thou badest me: arise, I pray thee, sit and eat of my venison, that thy soul may bless me."

22. "Now therefore be not grieved, nor angry with yourselves, that ye sold me hither: for God did send me before you to preserve life."

23. "I do not know the man."

24. "The woman whom thou gavest to be with me, she gave me of the tree, and I did eat."

25. "Behold, I have hearkened unto your voice in all that ye said unto me, and have made a king over you."

26. "One basket had very good figs, even like the figs that are first ripe: and the other basket had very naughty figs, which could not be eaten, they were so bad."

27. "I have sinned in that I have betrayed the innocent blood."

28. "Curse God, and die."

29. "What have I done unto thee, that thou hast smitten me these three times?"

30. "Go and search diligently for the young child; and when ye have found him, bring me word again, that I may come and worship him also."

ANSWERS

1. Cain. Genesis 4:9. 2. Ruth. Ruth 1:16. 3. Moses. Exodus 5:1. 4. David. II Samuel 18:33. 5. Jesus. Mark 15:34. 6. Samson. Judges 16:28. 7. Job. Job 1:21 8. Jonah. Jonah 1:12 9. Daniel. Daniel 6:22. 10. Nathan. II Samuel 12:7.

11. Solomon. I Kings 3:25. 12. Saul. I Samuel 22:13. 13. Sarah. Genesis 18:12. 14. Isaac. Genesis 22:7. 15. Eve. Genesis 3:13. 16. Esau. Genesis 25:30. 17. Joshua. Joshua 3:10. 18. Goliath. I Samuel 17:8–9. 19. Pontius Pilate. John 19:6. 20. Esther. Esther 8:5.

21. Jacob. Genesis 27:19. 22. Joseph. Genesis 45:5. 23. Peter. Matthew 26:72. 24. Adam. Genesis 3:12. 25. Samuel. I Samuel 12:1. 26. Jeremiah. Jeremiah 24:2. 27. Judas. Matthew 27:4. 28. Job's wife. Job 2:9. 29. Balaam's ass. Numbers 22:28. 30. Herod. Matthew 2:8.

BIBLE BY THE NUMBERS

■

"In a hundred years the Bible will be a forgotten book found only in museums," predicted French author Voltaire, writing from his home in Geneva. A century later his home was owned and occupied by the Geneva Bible Society.

The thirty-nine books of the Old Testament, the twenty-seven books of the New Testament, and the fifteen books of the Apocrypha compose the champion best-seller of all time. Translated into more than 2,000 languages, the Bible is available to about 80 percent of the world's people and outsells all other popular books. Each year in the United States alone, approximately 44 million copies are sold and 91 million distributed. Astonishingly, the average American home contains 6.8 Bibles.

With those vital statistics in mind, try your hand and memory at playing a numbers game about the Bible:

1. How many books of the Bible are named after women?
2. How many days did it take God to create the world?
3. How many times are the words *apple, snake,* and *whale* mentioned in the King James Bible versions of Genesis and Jonah?
4. How many rivers were there in Eden?
5. How long did Methuselah live?
6. How many cubits in length did God command Noah to build the ark?

7. How many of each animal went onto the ark?

8. How long did the flood last?

9. God agreed to spare Sodom and Gomorrah if Abraham could find how many righteous people there?

10. How old was Abraham when his son Isaac was born?

11. How many patriarchs were there?

12. How many brothers did Joseph have?

13. How many kine were in the dream that Pharaoh related to Joseph?

14. How many tribes of Israel were there?

15. How many plagues were visited on the Egyptians because Pharaoh would not let the people of Israel go?

16. How many years did Israel wander in the desert?

17. How many commandments did God deliver to Moses on Mount Sinai?

18. How many times did Balaam smite his ass?

19. How many days did Joshua and his army circle Jericho, blowing their trumpets at its walls?

20. How many men did Samson slay with the jawbone of an ass?

21. How long did Solomon rule over Israel?

22. How many wives and how many concubines did Solomon have?

23. How long did Jonah remain in the belly of the fish?

24. How many comforters did Job have?

25. According to the Psalms, how many years are allotted to each human being?

26. Which psalm begins, "The Lord is my shepherd; I shall not want. He maketh me to lie down in green pastures"?

27. Of how many beasts did Daniel dream?

28. How many friends of Daniel were cast into the fiery furnace but saved by God?

29. How many gospels are there in the Bible?

30. How many months older than Jesus was John the Baptist?

31. How many brothers did Jesus have?

32. How many apostles did Jesus recruit?

33. How many days did Jesus fast in the desert?

34. How many parables of Jesus are there in the Bible?

35. How many men did Jesus feed with how many loaves and how many fishes?

36. How many men passed by the injured man before the Samaritan stopped to help?

37. In the parable of the workers in the vineyard, at what hour were the last workers hired?

38. For how many days had Lazarus been dead before being raised by Jesus?

39. In Jesus's parable of the virgins, how many virgins were there? How many were wise and how many foolish?

40. By the end of the parable of the talents, how many talents had the man who had originally been given five?

41. How many Beatitudes did Jesus deliver?

42. With how many thieves was Jesus crucified?

43. How many hours did Jesus hang on the cross before he died?

44. How many pieces of silver were given for Judas's betrayal?

45. How many times did Peter deny Jesus?

46. How many Marys told of Jesus's resurrection?

47. How many days occurred between his death and his resurrection?

48. The Book of Revelation mentions a scroll closed with how many seals?

49. How many Horsemen of the Apocalypse were there?

50. What is the Number of the Beast?

ANSWERS

1. Two in the Old Testament—Ruth and Esther; two in the Apocrypha—Judith and Susanna. 2. Six. Genesis 1:31. 3. Zero. *Fruit, serpent,* and *great fish* are mentioned a number of times. 4. Four. Genesis 2:10. 5. 969 years. Genesis 5:27. 6. Three hundred. Genesis 6:15. 7. Two. Genesis 7:14–16. But note Genesis 7:2–3, which numbers the clean beasts and fowls of the air by sevens. 8. Forty days. Genesis 7:17. 9. Ten. Genesis 18:32. 10. One hundred years old. Genesis 21:5.

11. Three: Abraham, Isaac, and Jacob. 12. Eleven. Genesis 35:22. 13. Fourteen; seven fat and seven lean. Genesis 41:17–20. 14. Twelve. Genesis 49:28. 15. Ten. Exodus 7–11. 16. Forty. Joshua 5:6. 17. Ten. Exodus 20:3–17. 18. Three. Numbers 22:28. 19. Seven. Joshua 6:14–15. 20. A thousand. Judges 15:15.

21. Forty years. I Kings 11:42. 22. Seven hundred and three hundred. I Kings 11:3. 23. Three days and nights. Jonah 1:17. 24. Three. Job 2:11. 25. Seventy. Psalms 90:10. 26. The twenty-third. 27. Four. Daniel 7:3–7. 28. Three. Daniel 3:19. 29. Four. 30. Six. Luke 1:26.

31. Four: James, Joses, Juda, and Simon. Mark 6:3. 32. Twelve. Matthew 10:2. 33. Forty. Matthew 4:2. 34. Believe it or not, sixty-four. 35. Five thousand, with five loaves and two fishes. Mark 6:38 and 6:44, Luke 9:13, John 6:9–10. 36. Two. Luke 10:31–32. 37. The "eleventh hour." Matthew 20:6. 38. Four. John 11:17. 39. Ten: five wise and five foolish. Matthew 25:1–2. 40. Eleven. Matthew 25:28.

41. Nine. Matthew 5:3–11. 42. Two. Mark 15:27. 43. Six (from the third hour to the ninth hour). Matthew 15:25 and 15:34. 44. Thirty. Matthew 26:15, 27:3. 45. Three. Matthew 26:69–75. 46. Two: Mary Magdalene and Mary the mother of James. Luke 24:10. 47. Three. Matthew 27:63. 48. Seven. Revelation 5:1, 8:1. 49. Four. Revelation 6:2–8. 50. 666. Revelation 13:18.

BIBLE RIDDLES

■

Riddles are perhaps the most ancient of all verbal puzzles, dating back at least 2,500 years. The most famous riddle of all is the one that the Sphinx put to Oedipus: "What goes on four legs in the morning, on two at noon and on three at night?" Oedipus, one of the first game show contestants, answered the riddle correctly and thus became Oedipus Rex. His solution: "Man: in infancy, he crawls; in his prime, he walks; in old age, he leans on a staff."

In the biblical Book of Judges, the mighty Samson comes upon a swarm of bees making honey in the carcass of a lion. From this, Samson makes a bet with the Philistines that they cannot solve his original riddle: "Out of the eater came forth meat, and out of the strong came forth sweetness." After seven days of weeping, Samson's wife wheedles the answer out of him and conveys it to the Philistines. In a rage, Samson kills thirty of them and lays waste their city. Today we don't take riddles quite as seriously, but we do derive sweetness and strength from a cleverly turned poser.

The Bible has inspired not only an outpouring of great literature, art, and music, but also an impressive array of riddles based on its stories. The canon of biblical riddles reminds us that we can laugh with the Bible as well as learn from it:

1. When was baseball first played in the Bible?

2. What animals disobeyed God's command to "be fruitful and multiply"?

3. Who was the champion runner of all time?

4. What was the longest day in the Bible?

5. At what time of day was Adam created?

6. Why couldn't Eve have measles?

7. Did Eve ever have a date with Adam?

8. On what did the earliest people do arithmetic lessons?

9. How were Adam and Eve prevented from gambling?

10. What did Adam and Eve never have but left to their children?

11. What evidence is there that Adam and Eve were pretty noisy?

12. How long did Cain hate his brother?

13. When was meat first mentioned in the Bible?

14. What animal took the most baggage into the ark; what animals took the least?

15. Why weren't there any worms in the ark?

16. What creatures were not on the ark?

17. Where did Noah keep the bees?

18. Who was the best financier in the Bible?

19. Where did all the people in the world hear one rooster crow?

20. Why couldn't people play cards on the ark?

21. Where was Noah when the lights went out?

22. Why couldn't Noah catch many fish?

23. When is paper money first mentioned in the Bible?

24. What did the cat say when the ark landed?

25. Why was Lot's wife turned into a pillar of salt?

26. When was tennis first played?

27. Who was the straightest man in the Bible?

28. How was Pharaoh's daughter like a stockbroker?

29. What did the Egyptians do when it got dark?

30. Who was the first man in the Bible to break all ten commandments?

31. How do we know for certain that Moses was a male?

32. Who were the three most constipated men in the Bible?

33. Who was the greatest actor in the Bible? What did he die of?

34. How was Ruth rude to Boaz?

35. Why was Goliath astonished when David hit him with a stone?

36. Who was older—David or Goliath?

37. What evidence is there of sewing in the time of David?

38. Why was the prophet Elijah like a horse?

39. Who was the most successful doctor in the Bible?

40. What did Job have to cover his sackcloth and ashes?

41. Who was the strongest man in the Bible?

42. Who was Jonah's guardian?

43. How is the story of Jonah an inspiration?

44. How was John the Baptist like a penny?

45. Who were the three tiniest apostles?

46. Who set the record for the high jump in the Bible?

47. How was St. Paul like a horse?

48. How was a baseball game played in the Bible?

49. Who were the shortest men in the Bible?

50. What three noblemen are mentioned in the Bible?

ANSWERS

1. In the big inning. 2. adders 3. Adam. He was the first in the human race. 4. The one with no Eve. 5. A little before Eve.

6. Because she'd Adam. 7. No, it was an apple. 8. God told them to multiply on the face of the earth. 9. They lost their paradise. 10. Parents.

11. They raised Cain. 12. As long as he was Abel. 13. When Noah took Ham into the ark. 14. The elephant took his trunk,

but the fox and the rooster took only a brush and comb between them. 15. Because worms come in apples, not in pairs.

16. Fish. 17. In the ark hives. 18. Noah. He floated his stock while the whole world was in liquidation. 19. In the ark. 20. Noah sat on the deck.

21. In d'ark. 22. He only had two worms. 23. When the dove brought the green back to the ark. 24. Is that Ararat? 25. Because she was dissatisfied with her Lot.

26. When Joseph served in Pharaoh's court. 27. Joseph. Pharaoh made a ruler out of him. 28. She took a little prophet from the rushes on the banks. 29. They turned on the Israelites. 30. Moses.

31. He wandered around the desert for forty years and never stopped to ask anyone for directions. 32. Cain, because he wasn't Abel; Methuselah, who sat on the throne for 900 years; and Moses, because God gave him two tablets and sent him into the wilderness. 33. Samson. He brought down the house, then died of fallen arches. 34. She pulled his ears and stepped on his corn. 35. It had never entered his head before.

36. David. He rocked Goliath to sleep. 37. He was hemmed in on all sides. 38. He was fed from aloft. 39. Job. He had the most patience. 40. Only three miserable comforters.

41. Jonah. The whale couldn't keep him down. 42. The whale brought him up. 43. Jonah was down in the mouth but came out all right. 44. He was one sent. 45. Peter, James, and John. They all slept on a watch.

46. Jesus, when he cleared the temple. 47. He liked Timothy, hey? 48. In the big inning, Eve stole first, Adam stole second, Rebecca walked with the pitcher, Gideon rattled the pitchers, Saul was put out by David, Absalom and Judas went out swinging, and the prodigal son stole home. 49. It is commonly believed that they were Knee-high Meyer and Bildad the Shuhite (shoe height), but Paul said, "Silver and gold have I none," and no one could be shorter than that. 50. Barren fig tree, Lord how long, and Count thy blessings.

IN THE BEGINNING
WAS A TITLE

∎

In John Steinbeck's novella *The Pearl,* the young Mexican diver, Kino, finds a magnificent pearl and with it tries to buy peace and happiness for his family. In both the title and the story, the author hopes that his readers will catch the connection between his classic fable and the parable of Jesus as told in Matthew 13:45–46: "The kingdom of heaven is like unto a merchant man, seeking goodly pearls, who, when he had found one pearl of great price, went and sold all that he had, and bought it." As a kind of elbow-in-the-ribs hint, Steinbeck writes in the epigraph, "If this story is a parable, perhaps everyone takes his own meaning from it."

A font of inspiration, wisdom, and stylistic beauty, the Bible is also a major source of literary titles. Identify the works that draw their titles from the following biblical passages. Also name each author:

1. One generation passeth away, and another generation cometh: but the earth abideth for ever. The sun also ariseth, and the sun goeth down, and hasteth to his place where he arose.— Ecclesiastes 1:4–5

2. And lead us not into temptation, but deliver us from evil: For thine is the kingdom, and the power, and the glory, for ever. Amen.—Matthew 6:13

3. My bone cleaveth to my skin and to my flesh, and I am escaped with the skin of my teeth.—Job 19:20

4. O my son Absalom, my son, my son Absalom! would God I had died for thee, O Absalom, my son, my son!—II Samuel 18:33

5. The Lord is my shepherd; I shall not want. He maketh me to lie down in green pastures: he leadeth me beside the still waters. He restoreth my soul.—Psalms 23:1–3

6. I have been a stranger in a strange land.—Exodus 2:22

7. He that troubleth his own house shall inherit the wind: and the fool shall be servant to the wise at heart.—Proverbs 11:29

8. Let us now praise famous men, and our fathers who begat us.—Ecclesiasticus 44:1

9. O generation of vipers, who hath warned you to flee from the wrath to come?—Matthew 3:7

10. So he drove out the man; and he placed at the east of the garden of Eden Cherubims, and a flaming sword which turned every way, to keep the way of the tree of life.—Genesis 3:24

11. That ye may be the children of your Father which is in heaven: for he maketh his sun to rise on the evil and on the good, and sendeth rain on the just and on the unjust.—Matthew 5:45

12. I looked, and behold a pale horse; and his name that sat on him was Death.—Revelation 6:8

13. There were giants in the earth in those days.—Genesis 6:4

14. The young lions roar after their prey, and seek their meat from God.—Psalms 104:21

15. By the rivers of Babylon, there we sat down, yea, we wept, when we remembered Zion.—Psalms 137:1

16. Consider the lilies of the field, how they grow; they toil not, neither do they spin.—Matthew 6:28

ANSWERS

1. *The Sun Also Rises*, Ernest Hemingway 2. *The Power and the Glory*, Graham Greene 3. *The Skin of Our Teeth*, Thornton Wilder 4. *Absalom, Absalom!*, William Faulkner 5. *The Green Pastures*, Marc Connelly 6. *Stranger in a Strange Land*, Robert Heinlein 7. *Inherit the Wind*, Jerome Lawrence and Robert E. Lee 8. *Let Us Now Praise Famous Men*, James Agee 9. *Generation of Vipers*, Philip Wylie 10. *East of Eden*, John Steinbeck

11. *The Just and the Unjust*, James Gould Cozzens 12. *Pale Horse, Pale Rider*, Katherine Anne Porter 13. *Giants in the Earth*, O. E. Rölvaag 14. *The Young Lions*, Irwin Shaw 15. "By the Waters of Babylon," Stephen Vincent Benét 16. *The Lilies of the Field*, William E. Barrett

GOOD WORDS
FROM THE GOOD BOOK

■

While the spiritual values of the Bible are almost universally recognized, the enduring effect of the Bible on the English language is often overlooked. The fact is, though, that a great number of biblical words, references, and expressions have become part of our everyday speech, and even people who don't read the Bible carry its text on their tongues.

Here are a dozen biblically inspired words, each of which you are asked to identify:

1. In ancient times, a _____ was a unit of weight, and this weight of silver or gold constituted a monetary unit, one that figures prominently in a famous parable of Jesus: "For the kingdom of heaven is as a man travelling into a far country, who called his own servants, and delivered unto them his goods. And unto one he gave five _____, to another two, and to another one; to every man according to his several ability." (Matthew 25:14–15)

The most common modern meaning of the word _____ — some special, often God-given ability or aptitude—is a figurative development from the parable.

2. An obstacle: "Thou shalt not curse the deaf, nor put a_____before the blind, but shalt fear thy God." (Leviticus 19:14)

3. A special celebration: "And ye shall hallow the fiftieth year, and proclaim liberty throughout all the land unto all the inhabitants thereof: it shall be a_____unto you." (Leviticus 25:10)

4. "Now when Jesus was risen early the first day of the week, he appeared first to Mary Magdalene, out of whom he had cast seven devils. And she went and told them that had been with him, as they mourned and wept." (Mark 16:9–10) Mary Magdalene became a favorite subject of medieval and Renaissance painters, who traditionally depicted her as weeping. The tearful Mary was portrayed so sentimentally that, over the years, her name has been transformed into the word_____, which has come to mean "tearfully sentimental."

5. One to whom some form of blame or guilt is transferred: "And Aaron shall cast lots upon the two goats; one lot for the Lord, and the other lot for the_____... the goat, on which the lot fell to be the_____, shall be presented alive before the Lord, to make an atonement with him, and to let him go for a_____into the wilderness." (Leviticus 16:8–10)

According to Leviticus, the original_____was an actual goat upon whose head was symbolically placed all the sins of the community. The animal was allowed to escape into the wilderness, carrying the tremendous burden of sin with it and thus relieving the people.

6. A final, decisive battle, marked by overwhelming slaughter: "And he gathered them together into a place called in the Hebrew tongue_____... And there were voices, and thunders, and lightnings; and there was a great earthquake, such as was not since men were upon the earth, so mighty an earthquake, and so great." (Revelation 16:16,18)

7. Anything of enormous size: "Behold now_____, which I made with thee ... Behold, he drinketh up a river and hasteth

not: he trusteth that he can draw up Jordan into his mouth." (Job 40:15, 23).

8. Anything of enormous size: "In that day the Lord with his sore and great and strong sword shall punish_____the piercing serpent, even_____that crooked serpent; and he shall slay the dragon that is in the sea." (Isaiah 27:1)

9. "How doth the city sit solitary, that was full of people! How is she become as a widow! She that was great among the nations, and princess among the provinces, how is she become tributary!"

This is a typically dark passage in one of the prophetic books, from which we derive the word_____, meaning a sorrowful tirade, extended lament, or bitter denunciation.

10. "Then the Lord of the_____gathered them together for to offer a great sacrifice unto Dagon their god, and to rejoice." (Judges 16:23)

Because the nation described above were an alien, non-Semitic people who worshiped strange gods, their name became a term for a foreigner. Nineteenth-century philosophers, such as Thomas Carlyle and Matthew Arnold, further changed the meaning of the word so that today_____is a derogatory term for one who shuns intellectual and cultural activities.

11. In Judges 12:5–6, we learn about a conflict between the peoples of Gilead and Ephraim: "And the Gileadites took the passages of Jordan before the Ephraimites: and it was so, that when those Ephraimites which were escaped said, Let me go over; that the men of Gilead said unto him, Art thou an Ephraimite? If he said, Nay; Then they said unto him, Say now_____" (Judges 12:5–6).

Because the Ephraimites didn't have the *sh* sound in their language, they could not pronounce the word correctly, and 42,000 of them were slain. That's how the word_____has acquired the meaning that it has today: a password, catchword, or slogan that distinguishes one group from the other.

12. "Then the Lord rained upon_____and upon Gomorrah

brimstone and fire from the Lord out of heaven." (Genesis 19:24) Because of the wicked and unnatural practices of its citizens, that city's name gives us the word_____, which describes various forms of "unnatural" sexual acts.

ANSWERS

1. talent 2. stumbling block 3. jubilee 4. maudlin 5. scapegoat 6. armageddon 7. behemoth 8. leviathan 9. jeremiad 10. philistine 11. shibboleth 12. sodomy

HOLY MOSES!

∎

Along with the works of William Shakespeare, the King James Bible is the most fruitful source of everyday phrases in the English-speaking world. Exclamations like "Holy Moses!" and "Judas Priest!" are the most obvious, but there are dozens of other biblical phrases that season our speech.

Many such expressions are direct borrowings, such as "kingdom come," in Matthew 6:10, and "the eleventh hour," from Matthew's version of Jesus's parable of the workers in the vineyard who gained employment so late in the day (Matthew 20:6).

Others have entered our modern idiom in a slightly revised form, as "crystal clear" (from "clear as crystal" in Revelation 22:1) and "by the skin of my teeth." The latter echoes Job's lament in Job 19:20: "My bone cleaveth to my skin and to my flesh, and I am escaped with the skin of my teeth" ("by the skin of my teeth" in the Revised Standard Version). "But teeth don't have any skin," you protest. In the biblical phrase, the "skin" refers to a margin of safety as thin as the enamel on the teeth.

In the Song of Solomon 7:4, the beloved is told, "Thy neck is as a tower of ivory." From this comparison derives the modern cliché "an ivory tower," which picks up the sense of beauty, loftiness, and unassailability implied by the original words.

Still other expressions are general references to a biblical story, like "to raise Cain" and "Adam's apple," so called because many men, but few women, exhibit a bulge of laryngeal cartilage in front of their throats. According to male-dominated folklore, Eve swallowed her apple without care or residue, while a chunk of the fruit stuck in the throat of the innocent and misled Adam.

Here, listed in the order they occur in the Bible, are fifty biblical turns of phrase that have survived the centuries pretty much unscathed. Complete each item:

1. Saw the_____(Genesis 1:4)
2. My brother's_____(Genesis 4:9)
3. Sold his_____for a mess of_____(Genesis 25:33–34)
4. The_____of the land (Genesis 45:18)
5. A land flowing with_____and_____(Exodus 3:17)
6. Man doth not live by_____alone (Deuteronomy 8:3)
7. The_____of his eye (Deuteronomy 32:10)
8. A hair's_____(Judges 20:16)
9. A man after his own_____(I Samuel 13:14)
10. Played the_____(I Samuel 26:21)
11. A still small_____(I Kings 19:12)
12. Weeping and_____(Esther 4:3)
13. Give up the_____(Job 3:11)
14. In the land of the_____(Job 28:13)
15. Out of the mouths of_____(Psalms 8:2)
16. His heart's_____(Psalms 10:3)
17. At their wit's_____(Psalms 107:27)
18. Labor in_____(Psalms 127:1)
19. Out of the_____(Psalms 130:1)
20. Pride goeth . . . before a_____(Proverbs 16:18)
21. Vanity of_____(Ecclesiastes 1:2)
22. There is nothing new under the_____(Ecclesiastes 1:9)
23. Eat, drink, and be_____(Ecclesiastes 8:15)
24. As white as_____(Isaiah: 1:18)
25. They shall beat their_____into_____(Isaiah 2:4)
26. Woe is_____! (Isaiah 6:5)
27. See eye to_____(Isaiah 52:8)
28. Holier than_____(Isaiah 65:5)

29. Weighed in the_____(Daniel 5:27)

30. Salt of the_____(Matthew 5:13)

31. Good for_____(Matthew 5:13)

32. An eye for an_____, and a tooth for a_____(Matthew 5:38; cf. Exodus 21:24)

33. Pearls before_____(Matthew 7:6)

34. House_____against itself (Matthew 12:25)

35. Fell by the_____(Matthew 13:4)

36. Signs of the_____(Matthew 16:3)

37. A den of_____(Matthew 21:13)

38. Blood_____(Matthew 27:6)

39. In his right_____(Mark 5:15)

40. Physician,_____thyself (Luke 4:23)

41. A law unto_____(Romans 2:14)

42. The powers that_____(Romans 13:1)

43. It is high_____(Romans 13:11)

44. In the twinkling of an_____(I Corinthians 15:52)

45. A_____in the flesh (II Corinthians 12:7)

46. Labor of_____(I Thessalonians 1:3)

47. The root of all_____(I Timothy 6:10)

48. Keep the_____(II Timothy 4:7)

49. Cover a_____of sins (I Peter 4:8)

50. Bottomless_____(Revelation 9:1, 20:1)

ANSWERS

1. light 2. keeper 3. birthright, pottage 4. fat 5. milk, honey 6. bread 7. apple 8. breadth 9. heart 10. fool

11. voice 12. wailing 13. ghost 14. living 15. babes 16. desire 17. end 18. vain 19. depths 20. fall

21. vanities 22. sun 23. merry 24. snow 25. swords, plowshares 26. me 27. eye 28. thou 29. balances 30. earth

31. nothing 32. eye, tooth 33. swine 34. divided 35. wayside 36. times 37. thieves 38. money 39. mind 40. heal

41. themselves 42. be 43. high 44. eye 45. thorn 46. love 47. evil 48. faith 49. multitude 50. pit

THE BIBLE IN THE NEWS I

■

A front-page story in a St. Louis newspaper reported an incident in which two men were hospitalized after a fistfight. An automobile had stopped for a red light at a main intersection. A man on the sidewalk called out to its driver, "Hey, mister, your left front tire is going flat." The driver got out, looked at the tire, and called to his benefactor, "Thanks for being a good Samaritan!" Whereupon the pedestrian leaped off the curb and started pounding the driver with his fists, shouting, "You can't call me a dirty name!" The shocked driver struck back, and the result was that both men ended up in the hospital—all because one of them thought that "Samaritan" was an obscenity.

Few of us will end up eating a knuckle sandwich because we miss the source of a literary allusion—in this case, Luke 10:30–37. But our lives are considerably enriched when we are able to identify such sources, because allusions become keys that unlock the doors to many mansions—itself a biblical reference to John 14:2, where Jesus says, "In my Father's house are many mansions."

The following quotations drawn from news stories all allude to the Bible. As specifically as you can, identify the source of each allusion:

1. A 1983 Philadelphia 76ers championship banner proclaimed, "Moses Parts the Lakers."

2. Jesse Jackson declared that the [Democratic] party needed new wineskins to hold new wine.

3. The Mets should eat, drink, and be merry this winter because, based on recent history, once the next pennant race begins, they will die.

4. Vanessa Williams made at least two mistakes: posing for the photographer and posing for the pageant. She lost the balance you need to wear this commercial crown. But let him who has never turned a *Playboy* magazine to the centerfold cast the first stone.

5. George Hamilton has never been one to hide his enthusiasm under a bushel basket.

6. I was sick and tired of January and sick and tired of February following after January year after year like famine and pestilence following war.

7. Each town has about a hundred Doubting Thomases and about four visionaries.

8. The only thing you need to be a successful farmer these days is faith, hope and parity.

9. On tennis player John McEnroe: "Mac the Strife is a man who hasn't followed the biblical precept to put away childish things. He is a sniveling whiner. If he can't have everything his way, he throws a tantrum."

10. The first were last and the last were first in the opening round of the 33rd Beanpot Hockey Tournament.

ANSWERS

1. In Exodus 14:1–31, Moses parted the waters of the Red Sea, and the Israelites passed through safely while the Egyptians pursuing them were drowned. On the banner, Moses refers to

center Moses Malone and the Lakers to the Los Angeles Lakers. 2. In Matthew 9:17, Jesus advises, "Neither do men put new wine into old bottles: else the bottles break, and the wine runneth out, and the bottles perish: but they put new wine into new bottles, and both are preserved." 3. In I Corinthians 15:32, Paul writes, "Let us eat and drink; for tomorrow we die." 4. When a crowd wishes to stone an adulterous woman, Jesus says, "He that is without sin among you, let him first cast a stone at her." (John 8:7) 5. Jesus advises that the good things of life should not be hidden: "Neither do men light a candle, and put it under a bushel." (Matthew 5:15, Mark 4:21, Luke 11:33)

6. Famine and pestilence are linked in several places in the Bible, including Ezekiel 6:11: "They shall fall by the sword, by the famine, and by the pestilence." 7. After Jesus's resurrection, the disciple Thomas said, "Except I shall see in his hands the print of the nails, and put my finger into the print of the nails, and thrust my hand into his side, I will not believe." (John 20:24–29) 8. A clever pun on Paul's famous statement in I Corinthians 13:13: "And now abideth faith, hope, charity, these three; but the greatest of these is charity." 9. From the same epistle, 13:11: "When I was a child, I spake as a child, I understood as a child, I thought as a child: but when I became a man, I put away childish things." 10. Jesus preached that "many that are first shall be last; and the last shall be first." (Matthew 19:30, Mark 10:31)

THE BIBLE IN THE NEWS II

■

> *The steed bit his master;*
> *How came that to pass?*
> *He heard the good pastor*
> *Cry, "All flesh is grass."*

In this anonymous little poem, the horse chomps his master because of two errors of judgment. The misguided creature takes too literally the metaphor "All flesh is grass" and fails to recognize that the pastor was making an allusion, in this case to Isaiah 40:6–7: "All flesh is grass, and all the goodliness thereof is as the flower of the field: The grass withereth, the flower fadeth: because the spirit of the Lord bloweth upon it: surely the people is grass."

Churches and synagogues are not the only vessels in which biblical allusions abound. Because the Bible occupies such a central place in our culture, many news stories employ biblical references to make their points concisely and powerfully. Identify the biblical allusions in the following news stories:

1. One reason why the garment unions have so sedulously promulgated the slogan that man cannot live by bread alone may

be that they would prefer not to limit judgment of their worth to their successes in providing bread alone.

2. The fundamental import of her subsequent performances, including two more marathon world bests and a total of six New York wins, was that the race is to the swift. Never again would raw stamina win a woman's marathon.

3. [Manute] Bol always has the slightly bemused look on his face of the bewildered bushman in the movie *The Gods Must Be Crazy,* and like the bushman, he is very much a stranger in a strange land.

4. In Russia, hyperinflation, the worst scourge of all, threatens like some angry Goliath. But Yeltsin plays David badly: He lacks the political muscle and the fiscal and monetary tools to attack this crippling giant.

5. Politically, Helmut Schmidt has now come perilously close to being a voice crying in the wilderness.

6. For everything there is a season, including one for "coming out," the custom whereby young women are presented to that privileged class called "society."

7. "The world's finest makers of swords can and will be the world's finest makers of plowshares," the president told enthusiastic workers at a Westinghouse Electronic Corporation plant, one day before the scheduled announcement of a new round of base closings.

8. Now, without being quite ready to lie down like the lion with the lamb, these business and labor leaders say they want to work together for the national interest.

9. Whether Peter Ueberroth is worthy of the most important job in America, we shall see. Many are called as spiritual leaders, but few are chosen.

10. In Washington last week he [deposed Sudanese prime minister, Gaafar Al-Nimeirz] received a record 17 million dollars in economic aid, but at home Mr. Nimeirz reaped a whirlwind.

11. From any human perspective it [a terrorist attack aboard

an airplane] was horrible. But the terrorists didn't win either. Whether that's worth it in terms of deterrence, of discouraging future terrorists, that takes a Solomon-like judgment.

12. Dole beat Bush two-to-one in Iowa and cut Bush's New Hampshire lead in half in eight days. But Bush, listed as terminal, has become Lazarus.

13. To be fair, Bush could hardly have seen the tumultuous events coming. Who did? This [the Berlin Wall] was a wall that came tumbling down without the help of Joshua.

14. Headline: "Computer People are Creating a Valley of Babble in California."

15. Headline for an article about vanity license plates: "All is Vanity."

ANSWERS

1. "Man doth not live by bread only, but by every word that proceedeth out of the mouth of the Lord doth man live" (Deuteronomy 8:3) 2. Ecclesiastes 9:11 tells us that "the race is not to the swift, nor the battle to the strong." 3. "I have been a stranger in a strange land." (Exodus 2:22) 4. David slays the giant Goliath with a slingshot. (I Samuel 17:4–54) 5. "The voice of him that crieth in the wilderness, Prepare ye the way of the Lord." (Isaiah 40:3)

6. "To every thing there is a season, and a time to every purpose under the heaven." (Ecclesiastes 3:1) 7. The passage in Isaiah 2:4, "they shall beat their swords into plowshares, and their spears into pruning hooks," has become an emblem for valuing harmony above war. 8. "The wolf also shall dwell with the lamb, and the leopard shall lie down with the kid; and the calf and the young lion and the fatling together." (Isaiah 11:6) 9. In the parables of the workers in the vineyard and the marriage feast, Jesus explains that "many are called, but few are chosen." (Matthew 20:16, 22:14) 10. In one of the most powerful meta-

phors in the Bible, Hosea (8:7) warns that the enemies of God "have sown the wind, and they shall reap the whirlwind."

11. King Solomon was noted for the wisdom of his judgments, the most famous of which was a decision between two women who both claimed to be the mother of one infant. (I Kings 3:16–28) 12. Jesus raised Lazarus of Bethany from the dead. (John 11:38–44) 13. Joshua led the people in shouting and blowing their trumpets, and the walls of Jericho "fell down flat." (Joshua 6:20) 14. In Genesis 11:1–9, we learn of a Tower of Babel that was built to reach unto heaven. God scotches the project by fragmenting the language of the builders into many tongues. 15. The opening words of the Ecclesiastes preacher are "Vanity of vanities; all is vanity."

Mythology

TEST YOUR MYTHOLOGY IQ

■

Legend has it that Alexander the Great always carried a treasured edition of Homer and that he put it under his pillow at night, along with his sword. When Alexander defeated the Persian king Darius, a golden casket studded with gems was among the booty. Inside that chest Alexander placed his edition of Homer, proclaiming, "There is but one thing in life worthy of so precious a casket." Classical mythology is indeed a treasure trove of literature, philosophy, and religion.

Knock, knock.

Who's there?

Electrolux.

Electrolux who?

Electrolux her father, but not her mother.

You would have to possess a high mythological IQ to understand the humor of that little knock-knock joke, which is based on a reader's knowledge of Aeschylus's *Oresteia*. When Agamemnon, king of Greece, returned from the Trojan War, his wife, Clytemnestra, murdered him in his bath. Their daughter, Electra, who remained loyal to her father, sought a fatal revenge against her mother.

To see how powerful your mythological literacy is, we've prepared a test of Olympian proportions. The world of classical mythology is essentially a human world. Realizing how splendid

men and women could be, the Greeks and Romans made their
gods and goddesses in their own images. Match the items in
column three with each god and goddess in columns one and
two:

Greek name	Latin name	Realm
1. Zeus	Ceres	agriculture
2. Poseidon	Cupid	fire and the forge
3. Hades/Pluto	Diana	hearth and home
4. Hera	Dis	king of gods and men
5. Phoebus Apollo	Faunus	love
6. Pallas Athena	Juno	love and beauty
7. Ares	Jupiter/Jove	messenger of gods
8. Aphrodite	Liber	moon and the hunt
9. Hermes	Mars	nature
10. Hephaestus	Mercury	queen of gods
11. Artemis	Minerva	sea
12. Demeter	Neptune	sun
13. Hestia	Phoebus Apollo	underworld
14. Bacchus/Dionysus	Venus	war
15. Eros	Vesta	wine and revelry
16. Pan	Vulcan	wisdom

Now you are invited to hit a Homer. The following characters
were all involved in the events of the Trojan War, chronicled in
Homer's *Iliad* and other ancient works. Match each name in the
first column with the appropriate description in the second:

17. Achilles	king of Troy
18. Agamemnon	queen of Troy
19. Andromache	leader of Greek forces
20. Astyanax	chief warrior for the Greeks
21. Ajax	second greatest Greek warrior
22. Cassandra	mother of Achilles

23. Diomedes   best friend of Achilles
24. Hector   greatest Trojan warrior
25. Hecuba   wife of Hector
26. Helen   son of Hector
27. Iphigenia   "the face that launched a thousand ships"
28. Laocoön   daughter of Agamemnon
29. Menelaus   husband of Helen
30. Nestor   judge of beauty contest
31. Odysseus   Amazon killed by Achilles
32. Paris   first man to land at Troy
33. Patroclus   oldest and wisest of the Greeks
34. Penthesileia   feigned madness to avoid the war
35. Priam   went mad
36. Protesilaus   loud-voiced herald
37. Stentor   warned Trojans of Trojan horse
38. Thetis   prophetess to whom no one listened

The following characters are all involved in Homer's *Odyssey*.
Match each name in the first column with the appropriate description in the second:

39. Aeolus   hero of the *Odyssey*
40. Antinous   wife of Odysseus
41. Argus   son of Odysseus
42. Calypso   beautiful, dangerous witch
43. Circe   nymph who loved Odysseus
44. Odysseus   Odysseus's dog
45. Penelope   Theban prophet
46. Polyphemus   fatal singers
47. Scylla   arrogant suitor
48. Sirens   king of the winds
49. Telemachus   had 20/ vision
50. Tiresias   sea monster

Now let's move from individuals to classical couples. Match each mythological man with each mythological woman:

51. Aeneas	Clytemnestra
52. Agamemnon	Dido
53. Deucalion	Deianeira
54. Hades	Echo
55. Hercules	Eurydice
56. Narcissus	Galatea
57. Oedipus	Jocasta
58. Orpheus	Persephone
59. Pygmalion	Pyrrha
60. Pyramus	Thisbe

Become a groupie of mythic proportions by matching each trio with its collective name:

61. Brontes, Steropes, Arges	Cyclopes
62. Clotho, Lachesis, Atropos	Fates
63. Aglaia, Thalia, Euphrosyne	Furies
64. Tisiphone, Alecto, Megaera	Graces/Charites
65. Parthenope, Ligea, Leucosia	Sirens

ANSWERS

1. Jupiter/Jove, king of gods and men 2. Neptune, sea 3. Dis, underworld 4. Juno, queen of gods 5. Phoebus Apollo, sun 6. Minerva, wisdom 7. Mars, war 8. Venus, love and beauty 9. Mercury, messenger of gods 10. Vulcan, fire and the forge

11. Diana, moon and the hunt 12. Ceres, agriculture 13. Vesta, hearth and home 14. Liber, wine and revelry 15. Cupid, love 16. Faunus, nature

17. chief warrior for the Greeks 18. leader of Greek forces 19. wife of Hector 20. son of Hector

21. went mad 22. prophetess to whom no one listened

23. second greatest Greek warrior 24. greatest Trojan warrior
25. queen of Troy 26. "the face that launched a thousand ships"
27. daughter of Agamemnon 28. warned Trojans of Trojan
horse 29. husband of Helen 30. oldest and wisest of the Greeks

31. feigned madness to avoid the war 32. judge of beauty
contest 33. best friend of Achilles 34. Amazon killed by Achilles
35. king of Troy 36. first man to land at Troy 37. loud-voiced
herald 38. mother of Achilles

39. king of the winds 40. arrogant suitor 41. Odysseus's dog
42. nymph who loved Odysseus 43. beautiful, dangerous witch
44. hero of the *Odyssey* 45. wife of Odysseus 46. had 20/ vision
47. sea monster 48. fatal singers 49. son of Odysseus 50. Theban
prophet

51. Dido 52. Clytemnestra 53. Pyrrha 54. Persephone
55. Deianeira 56. Echo 57. Jocasta 58. Eurydice 59. Galatea
60. Thisbe

61. Cyclopes 62. Fates 63. Graces 64. Furies 65. Sirens

THERE'S A GOD
IN YOUR SENTENCE

■

Of all the literary sources that feed into our English language, mythology is one of the richest. We who are alive today constantly speak and hear and write and read the names of the ancient gods and goddesses and heroes and heroines, even if we don't always know it.

Echo, for example, is an echo of a story that is more than two millennia old. Echo was a beautiful nymph who once upon a time aided Zeus in a love affair by keeping Hera, his wife, occupied in conversation. As a punishment for such verbal meddling, Hera confiscated Echo's power to initiate conversation, allowing her to repeat only the last words of anything she heard.

Such was a sorry-enough fate, but later Echo fell madly in love with an exceedingly handsome Greek boy, Narcissus, who, because of Echo's peculiar handicap, would have nothing to do with her. So deeply did the nymph grieve for her unrequited love, that she wasted away until nothing was left of her but her voice, always repeating the last words she heard.

The fate that befell Narcissus explains why his name has been transformed into words like *narcissism* and *narcissistic,* pertaining to extreme self-love. One day Narcissus looked into a still forest lake and beheld a face reflected in the water. Not knowing that the face was his own, he at once fell in love with the beautiful image just beneath the surface, and he, like Echo, pined away for a love that could never be consummated.

Using the following descriptions, identify the gods and goddesses, heroes and heroines, and fabulous creatures that inhabit the world of classical mythology and the words that echo them:

1. One of the vilest of mythology's villains was a king who served the body of his young son to the gods. They soon discovered the king's wicked ruse, restored the dead boy to life, and devised a punishment to fit the crime. They banished the king to Hades, where he is condemned to stand in a sparkling pool of water with boughs of luscious fruit overhead; when he stoops to drink, the water drains away through the bottom of the pool, and when he wishes to eat, the branches of fruit sway just out of his grasp. Ever since, when something presents itself temptingly to our view, we invoke this king's name.

2. An adjective that means "merry, inspiring mirth" comes from the name the ancient Romans gave to the king of their gods because it was a happy omen to be born under his influence.

3. The frenetic Greek nature god was said to cause sudden fear by darting out from behind bushes and frightening passersby. That fear now bears his name.

4. The goddess of love and beauty gives us many words from both her Greek and Roman names.

5. A Greek herald in Homer's *Iliad* was a human public-address system, for his voice could be heard all over camp. Today, the adjective form of his name means "loud-voiced, bellowing."

6. The most famous of all of Homer's creations spent ten years after the fall of Troy wandering through the ancient world encountering sorceresses and cyclopses (with 20/ vision). The wily hero's name lives on in the word we use to describe a long journey or voyage marked by bizarre turns of events.

7. The hero Odysseus was tempted by mermaids who perched on rocks in the sea and lured ancient mariners to their deaths. Their piercing call has given us our word for the rising and falling whistle emitted by ambulances, fire engines, and police cars.

8. Another great Greek hero needed all his power to complete twelve exceedingly laborious labors. We use a form of his name to describe a mighty effort or an extraordinarily difficult task.

9. A tribe of female warriors cut off their right breasts in order to handle their bows more efficiently. The name of their tribe originally meant "breastless"; it now means a strong woman.

10. Because of its fluidity and mobility, quicksilver is identified by a more common label that is the Roman name for Hermes, the winged messenger of the gods. That name has also bequeathed us an adjective meaning "swift, eloquent, volatile."

ANSWERS

1. Tantalus—tantalize 2. Jove—jovial 3. Pan—panic 4. Aphrodite—aphrodisiac, hermaphrodite; Venus—venereal, venerate 5. Stentor—stentorian 6. Odysseus—odyssey 7. the Sirens—siren 8. Hercules—herculean 9. Amazons—amazon 10. Mercury—mercury, mercurial

MYTHOLOGY IN THE NEWS

■

In the comic strip "Wee Pals," one boy remarks to another, "The Romans were real groovy people, Ralph." Ralph answers, "Oh yeah? Just name one outstanding accomplishment of the Romans."

"Well," answers the first boy, "they understood Latin."

Another magnificent accomplishment of the Romans is that they also created myths, building on stories they inherited from Greek civilization. Millennia later, images from classical mythology suffuse even our newspapers and magazines.

The quotations that follow were written during the past fifteen years, and all draw from the fountainhead of mythology. As specifically as you can, identify the source of each allusion:

1. The [New York football] Giants, like Sisyphus's boulder, have dashed the hopes of their faithful and, at times, fanatical fans for all but two of the last 19 years.

2. Such soaring rates of inflation are so new that a retiree would have needed the foresight of a Cassandra to prepare for the consequences.

3. At the same time, a variety of baby-girl dolls were born like Athena from the head of Zeus—or the head of the toy corporation.

4. Evidently, AIDS viruses can sequester themselves inside macrophages soon after infection, before antibodies are made. In this way, Gendelman told a meeting sponsored by the Cancer Research Institute of New York, the microphage acts as a "Trojan Horse" for AIDS viruses, hiding and even transporting them around the body.

5. After 30 years with the [Baltimore] Orioles, Cal Ripken was finally named manager for the 1987 season. His loyalty has been a match for Penelope's.

6. As political actors, we must, like the contemplatives before us, delve to the bottom of the world, and, Atlas-like, we must take the world on our shoulders.

7. For all his glittering numbers, [basketball coach] Boeheen's Achilles' heel, much like Ray Meyer's and Lefty Driesell's before him, has been Syracuse's inconsequential showing in the NCAA's.

8. The Mets, sporting the best record in baseball, have demonstrated a Hydra-like ability to replace missing parts just as quickly as they're lost.

9. Now is the time to head off a dangerous, expensive, and futile new competition in space. But President Reagan has been Icarus pursuing the dream of mastering space.

10. Watching last weekend's two wild-card playoff games summoned stentorian echoes of Vince Lombardi.

11. Molly McGrath [played by Goldie Hawn] is like Circe in reverse, turning pigs into men.

12. "We surely felt we couldn't build those luxury boxes with that sword of Damocles hanging over our heads," Alioto said.

13. As for the idea that [Miami Dolphins coach Don] Shula is [star quarterback Dan] Marino's Pygmalion, the Dolphins coach laughs and reminds everyone that Marino is not your ordinary lump of clay.

14. Quoth the coach of a dreadful football team that has won hardly a game in three years, "I feel like Job. I'd rather be the phoenix rising from the ashes, but the ashes keep piling up."

15. Headline: "Nuclear Industry Opens Pandora's Box of Waste."

Answers

1. In classical mythology Sisyphus is condemned to eternal punishment in the underworld, where he rolls a huge rock up a cliff, only to have it roll down again as he reaches the top. Now you know who was the first rock and roller. 2. Cassandra, daughter of the Trojan king, Priam, possessed an extraordinary ability to foretell disasters, although no one would heed her warnings. 3. Athena, daughter of Zeus, sprang fully armed from her father's head. 4. The Greeks sent a huge wooden horse to the Trojans as an offering to Athena, but inside were hiding a host of soldiers who emerged by night and overthrew the Trojan city. 5. During

Odysseus's long absence, Penelope promised the insistent suitors that she would choose from among them once she was done weaving a burial garment. But each night she would secretly undo what she had woven that same day.

6. Atlas was a Titan who bore the burden of the heavens on his shoulders. 7. Achilles' mother sought to make him invulnerable by dipping him in the river Styx. But she held him by the heel, which became the one part of him that was mortal. 8. The Hydra was a mythical beast with many heads, each of which possessed the power to grow back as two when chopped off. 9. Daedalus built wings to enable himself and his son Icarus to fly. Icarus soared too high, and the sun's heat melted the wax of the wings. The boy fell into the sea and was drowned. 10. Stentor was a loud-voiced Greek herald with the volume of fifty men.

11. In the *Odyssey,* Circe was a witch who turned men into pigs. 12. Damocles was a sycophantic hanger-on of Dionysius who was invited to share the luxury he so envied. At a great feast, Damocles had to sit beneath a sword hanging over his head by a thread or hair. 13. Pygmalion sculpted the statue of a beautiful woman. Aphrodite brought the statue to life, and she became Pygmalion's wife, Galatea. 14. The phoenix was a giant bird who had the ability to arise from its own cremated ashes. 15. Pandora ("woman of all gifts") opened a jar (a box in the popular mind), and out flew a myriad of plagues and evils.

' Shakespeare

TEST YOUR SHAKESPEARE IQ

■

Name a play written by Bartley Campbell. Of course you can't, nor can just about anyone else alive today. Yet Campbell (1843–1888) was a popular American playwright whose giant ego towered above his talent. His professional stationery depicted two portraits on the letterhead—Bartley Campbell on one side and William Shakespeare on the other—linked by the words "A friendly rivalry." Today Campbell, a legend in his own mind, is forgotten, while Shakespeare endures and prevails as the one big gun in the canon of English literature who has no rival.

William Shakespeare is the darling of readers, playgoers, and critics alike. The critical work directly about the Bard or in some way relevant to him could constitute a library, and in fact does: the superb 280,000-volume Folger Library in Washington, D.C. Even if you somehow devoured that collection, you would still have to read 3,000 new discussions of Shakespeare each year to keep up with the new scholarship.

As the Huntsman in *King Henry VI* says, "This way, my lord, for this way lies the game."

Here's an untrivial quiz on a far-from-trivial author. Supply the basic facts about Shakespeare's life and works that the following twenty questions ask for:

1. List the dates of Shakespeare's birth and death.

2. In what town and country was Shakespeare born?

3. Name the monarchs who reigned in Shakespeare's country during his lifetime.

4. Name Shakespeare's wife. "Mrs. Shakespeare" is not acceptable.

5. How many children did the Shakespeares have?

6. With what theater was Shakespeare most intimately connected?

7. What was the name of Shakespeare's acting company?

8. What is the importance of the following lines (in the original spelling)?:

> *Good frend for Jesus sake forbeare,*
> *To digg the dust encloased heare!*
> *Blest be ye man yt spares thes stones,*
> *And curst be he yt moves my bones.*

9. One of Shakespeare's contemporaries rightly foresaw the magnitude of the Bard's achievement when he wrote of Shakespeare: "He was not of an age, but for all time!" Name the writer of that sentence.

10. How many plays did Shakespeare write?

11. What are the three categories by which the plays are generally classified?

12. Into how many acts is each play traditionally divided?

13. In what verse form did Shakespeare write his plays?

14. What do we call the first edition of Shakespeare's collected works?

15. Some scholars believe that Shakespeare didn't write Shakespeare. Name three people who supposedly ghostwrote for the Bard.

16. How many sonnets are in Shakespeare's sonnet sequence?

17. How many lines are in a typical Shakespearean sonnet?

18. Identify the plays begun by each of the following lines:

    a. Now is the winter of our discontent
       Made glorious summer by this son of York;

    b. Two households, both alike in dignity,
       In fair Verona, where we lay our scene,
       From ancient grudge break to new mutiny,
       Where civil blood makes civil hands unclean.

    c. Hence! home, you idle creatures, get you home!
       Is this a holiday?

    d. If music be the food of love, play on,

    e. Who's there?

    f. When shall we three meet again?
       In thunder, lightning, or in rain?

19. Name the lover or wife of each of the following characters: a. Romeo; b. Antony; c. Petruchio; d. Benedick; e. Hamlet; f. Othello; g. Brutus; h. Henry V; i. Troilus; j. Touchstone; k. Ferdinand; l. Duke Orsino.

20. Name the Shakespearean heroes with whom each of the following enemies contended: a. Iago; b. Macduff; c. Laertes and Claudius; d. Hotspur; e. Octavius Caesar; f. Richmond; g. Brutus and Cassius.

As Belarius exclaims in *Cymbeline,* "The game is up!" It's now time to consult the answers.

ANSWERS

1. and 2. Shakespeare was baptized in Holy Trinity Church in the English village of Stratford-upon-Avon on April 26, 1564, and was probably born three days earlier. He died in Stratford on April 23, 1616. 3. Elizabeth I and James I. 4. Anne Hathaway. 5. Three: Susanna and the twins, Hamnet and Judith.

6. The Globe. 7. For most of his career, Shakespeare was a member of the Lord Chamberlain's Company, later known as the King's Men. 8. These words are the epitaph on Shakespeare's grave in the chancel of the Holy Trinity Church. 9. Ben Jonson. 10. Thirty-seven.

11. Tragedies, comedies, and histories. 12. Five. 13. Blank verse: unrhymed iambic pentameter. 14. the First Folio. 15. Candidates include Sir Walter Raleigh, the Earl of Oxford, Francis Bacon, Christopher Marlowe, and the Earl of Essex.

16. 154. 17. 14. 18. a. *Richard III;* b. *Romeo and Juliet;* c. *Julius Caesar;* d. *Twelfth Night;* e. *Hamlet;* f. *Macbeth.* 19. a. Juliet; b. Cleopatra; c. Katharina; d. Beatrice; e. Ophelia; f. Desdemona; g. Portia; h. Katharine; i. Cressida; j. Audrey; k. Miranda; l. Viola. 20. a. Othello; b. Macbeth; c. Hamlet; d. Prince Hal (Henry V); e. Antony; f. Richard III; g. Julius Caesar.

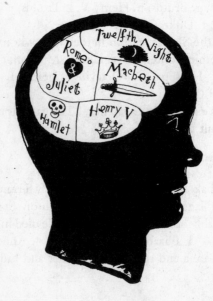

BOMB–BARD–MENT

Now that you've taken a fairly straightforward quiz about William Shakespeare, prepare yourself for some trick questions. Because these posers are fraught with snares, delusions, and arcane knowledge, do not expect to get many of them right. Still, we're confident that the answers will make fascinating reading:

1. What do the following sentences have in common?
>   We all make his praise.
>   I swear he's like a lamp.
>   "Has Will a peer?" I ask me.
>   Ah, I speak a swell rime.

2. What are Shakespeare's birth and death dates? How do they relate to St. George and Miguel de Cervantes?

3. Who is the Merchant of Venice?

4. In the famous balcony scene from *Romeo and Juliet,* Juliet says, "O Romeo, Romeo! wherefore art thou Romeo?" What does *wherefore* mean?

5. How many times does the word *witch* appear in the dialogue of *Macbeth*?

6. When Cleopatra's lover asked her if she was in love with

him, she answered, "Oh, Marc, I am!" Whether or not you caught the pun on "Omar Khayyám," correctly spell Marc's last name.

7. What character speaks the greatest number of lines in Shakespeare's plays?

8. What play contains the greatest number of Shakespearean lines? What play contains the smallest number?

9. What do these plays have in common?: *Love's Labour's Lost, The Taming of the Shrew, A Midsummer Night's Dream,* and *Hamlet*

10. What do these plays have in common?: *The Merchant of Venice, As You Like It, Twelfth Night,* and *Cymbeline*

11. "All the world's a stage . . . and one man in his_____plays many parts." Provide the missing word. In what play does this famous speech appear? Explain how in the same play a male plays a female who plays a male who plays a female.

12. So you think you know your Shakespeare and can quote his lines with exquisite accuracy? Examine these five Shakespearean quotations and provide the missing words:

    a. "Alas, poor Yorick! I knew him_____" (*Hamlet*)

    b. "To_____the lily" (*King John*)

    c. "All that_____is not gold" (*The Merchant of Venice*)

    d. "_____ will have his day" (*Hamlet*)

    e. "To the_____born" (*Hamlet*)

13. Are Shakespeare's sonnets addressed to a man or a woman?

14. What do the following words have in common?: *auspicious, bedroom, critic, dwindle, frugal, generous, majestic, obscene, submerge*

ANSWERS

1. Each of the four sentences is an anagram of WILLIAM SHAKESPEARE, and each uses all the letters in his name. 2. Shakespeare was almost certainly born on April 23—St. George's Day—in 1564, and he died on the same day fifty-two years later, the same day on which the Spanish writer Miguel de Cervantes died. 3. Antonio, not Shylock. 4. "Why," not "where." (Think about the cliché "the whys and wherefores.") Thus, the spoken stress should be placed on *Romeo*, not *art*. 5. Twice, I, 3, 6: "Aroint thee, witch!" and IV, 1, 23: "Witche's

mummy." While the word *witch* appears many times in the stage directions, the lines of the play generally refer to the witches as "weird sisters."

6. Antony, not Anthony. 7. With a total of 1,422 lines, an actor playing Hamlet has more to learn than one playing any other single part in a single play by Shakespeare. But the character who speaks the greatest number of lines in Shakespeare is Sir John Falstaff—1,178 in *Henry IV,* Parts I and II, and an additional 436 lines in *The Merry Wives of Windsor,* for a total of 1,614 lines. 8. *Hamlet,* with 3,931 lines, is the longest of Shakespeare's plays, and *The Comedy of Errors,* with 1,778, is the shortest. But the answer to the question of what play contains the smallest number of Shakespearean lines is not *The Comedy of Errors.* That's because Shakespeare collaborated with other playwrights on *Henry VIII* (to which he contributed 1,167 lines), *Pericles* (1,140 lines), and *The Two Noble Kinsmen,* which he wrote with John Fletcher and to which he contributed 1,131 lines. 9. Each play contains a play within a play. 10. Each play involves a woman who disguises herself as a man.

11. *Time,* not *life.* Most people say Hamlet, but it is Jaques who delivers this speech in *As You Like It* (Act II, scene 7). In the earliest productions of Shakespeare's plays, only men and boys were allowed into the theater companies. In *As You Like It,* a male played the part of Rosalind, who, in the story, flees to the Forest of Arden disguised as a young man, who then pretends to be a woman in order to help her paramour, Orlando, practice his wooing. 12. a. *Horatio,* not *well;* b. *paint,* not *gild;* c. *glisters,* not *glitters;* d. *dog,* not *every dog;* e. *manner,* not *manor.* 13. Both. Most were addressed to a young man, but approximately the last 20 percent were addressed to a woman. 14. They are among the more than 1,700 words first found in Shakespeare, who, "be-thump'd with words," (*King John*) was truly "a man of fire-new words" (*Love's Labour's Lost*).

A MAN OF MANY TITLES

■

William Shakespeare was a busy and prolific writer who, in twenty-five years, turned out thirty-seven long plays and co-authored several others. Still he still found time to provide titles for their books to generations of authors who return again and again to the well of his felicitous phrasing.

Take *Macbeth,* for example. Near the end of the play, Macbeth expresses his darkening vision of life: "It is a tale/Told by an idiot, full of sound and fury,/Signifying nothing." Centuries later, William Faulkner purloined a phrase from that speech for his novel *The Sound and the Fury,* which is indeed told by an idiot, Benjy Compson. Earlier in the play one of the witches chants, "By the pricking of my thumbs,/Something wicked this way comes." Agatha Christie plucked the first line and Ray Bradbury the second as titles of their best-sellers. Other steals from just the one play *Macbeth* include Robert Frost's "Out, Out—," Rose Macauley's *Told by an Idiot,* Ellis Middleton's *Vaulting Ambition,* Adrienne Rich's *Of Woman Born,* Ngaio Marsh's *Light Thickens,* Anne Sexton's *All My Pretty Ones,* Alistair MacLean's *The Way to Dusty Death,* Edward G. Robinson's *All Our Yesterdays,* Philip Barry's *Tomorrow and Tomorrow,* Malcolm Evans's *Signifying Nothing,* and John Steinbeck's *The Moon is Down.*

Clearly Shakespeare was one of the most generous souls who ever set quill to parchment. Although he himself was never granted a title, he freely granted titles to others. Identify the titles plucked from the following lines:

1. How beauteous mankind is! O brave new world
   That has such people in't!
   —*THE TEMPEST*, V, 1, 183

2. The ears are senseless that should give us hearing,
   To tell him his commandment is fulfill'd,
   That Rosencrantz and Guildenstern are dead.
   Where should we have our thanks?
   —*HAMLET*, V, 2, 369

3. Now is the winter of our discontent
   Made glorious summer by this son of York;
   And all the clouds that low'r'd upon our house
   In the deep bosom of the ocean buried.
   —*RICHARD III*, I, 1, 1

4. There are no tricks in plain and simple faith;
   But hollow men, like horses hot at hand,
   Make gallant show and promise of their mettle;
   —*JULIUS CAESAR*, IV, 2, 22

5. Art any more than a steward? Dost thou think because thou art virtuous there shall be no more cakes and ale?
   —*TWELFTH NIGHT*, II, 3, 114

6. When to the sessions of sweet silent thought
   I summon up remembrance of things past,
   I sigh the lack of many a thing I sought,
   And with old woes new wail my dear time's waste;
   —*SONNET XXX*

7. And Caesar's spirit, ranging for revenge,
   With Ate by his side come hot from hell,
   Shall in these confines with a monarch's voice
   Cry 'Havoc,' and let slip the dogs of war,
   —*JULIUS CAESAR*, III, 1, 270

8. What may this mean,
   That thou, dead corse, again in complete steel,
   Revisits thus the glimpses of the moon
   —*HAMLET*, I, 4, 51

9. The sun's a thief, and with his great attraction
   Robs the vast sea; the moon's an arrant thief,
   And her pale fire she snatches from the sun;
   —*TIMON OF ATHENS*, IV, 3, 436

10. Men at some time are masters of their fates;
    The fault, dear Brutus, is not in our stars,
    But in ourselves, that we are underlings.
    —*JULIUS CAESAR*, 1, 2, 139

ANSWERS

1. *Brave New World*, Aldous Huxley 2. *Rosencrantz and Guildenstern Are Dead*, Tom Stoppard 3. *The Winter of Our Discontent*, John Steinbeck 4. "The Hollow Men," T. S. Eliot 5. *Cakes and Ale*, W. Somerset Maugham

6. *Remembrance of Things Past*, Marcel Proust 7. *The Dogs of War*, Frederick Forsyth 8. *The Glimpses of the Moon*, Edith Wharton 9. *Pale Fire*, Vladimir Nabokov 10. *Dear Brutus*, James Barrie

NOT A PASSING PHRASE

∎

Oscar Wilde once quipped, "Now we sit through Shakespeare in order to recognize the quotations." Unrivaled in so many other ways in matters verbal, Shakespeare is unequaled as a phrasemaker. "All for one, one for all," and "not a creature was stirring—not even a mouse," wrote Alexandre Dumas in *The Three Musketeers* and Clement Clarke Moore in "A Visit From St. Nicholas." But Shakespeare said them first—"One for all, or all for one we gage" in *The Rape of Lucrece* and "not a mouse stirring" in *Hamlet*.

A student who attended a performance of *Hamlet* came away complaining that the play "was nothing more than a bunch of clichés." The reason for this common reaction is that so many of the memorable expressions in *Hamlet* have become proverbial. In that one play alone were born *brevity is the soul of wit; there's the rub; to thine own self be true; it smells to heaven; the very witching time of night; the primrose path; though this be madness, yet there is method in't; dog will have his day; the apparel oft proclaims the man; neither a borrower nor a lender be; frailty, thy name is woman; something is rotten in the state of Denmark; more honored in the breach than the observance; hoist with his own petar; the lady doth protest too much; to be, or not to be; sweets to the sweet; to the manner born; in my heart of heart; yeoman's service;* and *more in sorrow than in anger*.

Cudgel thy brains to complete these expressions that first saw the light in the other plays of William Shakespeare:

1. all the world's a_____(*As You Like It*, II, 7, 139)
2. as good_____would have it (*The Merry Wives of Windsor*, III, 5, 83)
3. the better part of valor is_____(*Henry IV*, Part I, V, 4, 120)
4. a blinking_____(*The Merchant of Venice*, II, 9, 54)
5. break the_____(*The Taming of the Shrew*, I, 2, 265)
6. breath'd his_____(*Henry VI*, Part III, V, 2, 40)
7. come full_____(*King Lear*, V, 3, 175)
8. the course of true love never did run_____(*A Midsummer Night's Dream*, I, 1, 134)
9. eaten me out of house and_____(*Henry IV*, Part II, II, 1, 74)
10. every_____a king (*King Lear*, IV, 6, 107)
11. for_____sake (*Henry VIII*, Prologue, 23)
12. a foregone_____(*Othello*, III, 3, 428)
13. the green-ey'd_____(*Othello*, III, 3, 166)
14. have seen better_____(*As You Like It*, II, 7, 120)
15. household_____(*Henry V*, IV, 3, 52)
16. if music be the food of love,_____(*Twelfth Night*, I, 1, 1)
17. infinite_____(*Antony and Cleopatra*, II, 2, 235)
18. an itching_____(*Julius Caesar*, IV, 3, 10 and 12)
19. laid on with a_____(*As You Like It*, 1, 2, 106)
20. laugh yourselves into_____(*Twelfth Night*, III, 2, 69)
21. lov'd not_____but too well (*Othello*, V, 2, 344)
22. masters of their_____(*Julius Caesar*, I, 2, 139)
23. melted into air, into thin_____(*The Tempest*, IV, 1, 150)
24. milk of human_____(*Macbeth*, I, 5, 17)
25. more sinn'd against than_____(*King Lear*, III, 2, 60)
26. neither rhyme nor_____(*The Comedy of Errors*, II, 2, 48)
27. not_____an inch (*The Taming of the Shrew*, Ind. 1, 14)
28. one fell_____(*Macbeth*, IV, 3, 219)
29. a pair of star-_____lovers (*Romeo and Juliet*, Prologue, 6)
30. parting is such sweet_____(*Romeo and Juliet*, II, 2, 184)
31. a plague a' both your_____(*Romeo and Juliet*, III, 1, 99)
32. pomp and_____(*Othello*, III, 3, 354)

33. a pound of_____(*The Merchant of Venice,* IV, 1, 307)

34. the quality of mercy is not_____(*The Merchant of Venice,* IV, 1, 184)

35. salad_____(*Antony and Cleopatra,* I, 5, 73)

36. short_____(*Richard III,* III, 4, 95)

37. a sorry_____(*Macbeth,* II, 2, 19)

38. [a] spotless_____(*Richard II,* I, 1, 178)

39. strange_____(*The Tempest,* II, 2, 40)

40. too much of a good_____(*As You Like It,* IV, 1, 123)

41. a tower of_____(*Richard III,* V, 3, 12)

42. uneasy lies the head that wears a_____(*Henry IV,* Part II, III, 1, 31)

43. the most unkindest_____of all (*Julius Caesar,* III, 2, 183)

44. wear my heart upon my_____(*Othello* I, 1, 64)

45. what_____these mortals be (*A Midsummer Night's Dream,* III, 2, 115)

46. what the_____ (*The Merry Wives of Windsor,* III, 2, 19)

47. what's done, is_____(*Macbeth,* III, 2, 12)

48. wild-goose_____(*Romeo and Juliet,* II, 4, 71)

49. with bated_____(*The Merchant of Venice,* I, 3, 124)

50. the world's mine_____(*The Merry Wives of Windsor,* II, 2, 3)

ANSWERS

1. stage 2. luck 3. discretion 4. idiot 5. ice 6. last 7. circle 8. smooth 9. home 10. inch

11. goodness 12. conclusion 13. monster 14. days 15. words 16. play on 17. variety 18. palm 19. trowel 20. stitches

21. wisely 22. fates 23. air 24. kindness 25. sinning 26. reason 27. budge 28. swoop 29. cross'd 30. sorrow

31. houses 32. circumstance 33. flesh 34. strain'd 35. days 36. shrift 37. sight 38. reputation 39. bedfellows 40. thing

41. strength 42. crown 43. cut 44. sleeve 45. fools 46. dickens 47. done 48. chase 49. breath 50. oyster

SHAKESPEARE IN THE NEWS

■

In the 1983 NCAA basketball finals, Jim Valvano's North Carolina Wolfpack faced a bigger and significantly more talented team of Houston Cougars, emblazoned by rising star Akeem Olajuwon. In the closing seconds, North Carolina forward Lorenzo Charles looped behind Olajuwon, took a pass, and jammed the ball in for the winning basket. Shortly after, a *Sports Illustrated* advertisement featured a photograph of the move with this headline: "The Stuff That Dreams are Made of."

The promo was a clever pun on a passage spoken by Prospero in Shakespeare's *The Tempest* (IV, 1, 156–158):

> *We are such stuff*
> *As dreams are made on; and our little life*
> *Is rounded with a sleep.*

Each quotation that follows alludes to Shakespeare. As specifically as you can, identify the source of each allusion:

1. Nothing became George Bush and Barbara Bush like their leaving office.
2. But as a comic [Carson] appears to believe that it is better a borrower than a lender be. (from an article about Johnny Carson's using material from David Letterman)

3. And every time the Knicks drew close to the Bulls, Jordan did something that, like star-crossed lovers, brought them farther apart.

4. This is the first time that Bush has portrayed himself as more sinned against than sinning, when it comes to the volatile question of race.

5. Somebody had to suffer the slings and arrows and back-hands of Martina Navratilova and Chris Evert-Lloyd while Wimbledon marks time until Martina and Chris get their hands on each other tomorrow.

6. Out, Damned Despot (title of a magazine story about Ferdinand Marcos)

7. They came not to praise John Sununu, but to puree him.

8. [Peter] Ueberroth hangs over these negotiations like the ghost of Banquo. (from a story during the short-lived baseball strike of 1985)

9. "In the last four years we've created six million new jobs!" cries the Great Communicator, and the rabble hiss and clap their chopped hands and throw up their sweaty nightcaps.

10. Put another way, Qadaffi's madness is his method, so, at least in theory, he is a man with whom a determined adversary can do business.

11. If it is sleep that knits up the raveled sleeve of care, then an overwhelming number of Americans are walking around with distinctly tatty shirtcuffs.

12. To do well in New Hampshire, [Pat Robertson] would have to buck the independence of an electorate that has always shown skepticism for people who wear their religion on their sleeve.

13. To define pressure, he hearkens back to his days as president of Yale University and a prolonged, bitter strike that divided that New Haven, Connecticut, campus. There, Giamatti said, "plenty of things happened in a very concentrated community that aren't necessarily cakes and ale."

14. Schroeder, Kirkpatrick, and Elizabeth Dole have all bad-

mouthed the job [of president] and the possibility. We hope the ladies have protested too much. All have the experience to be considered for the job.

15. José Canseco is just trying to enjoy spring after a winter of discontent.

16. Salad Days are Past for Budmen (headline about a local hockey team called the Budmen)

17. The Governor, the Convict, and the Quality of Mercy (headline of a newspaper story about a governor and a convict on death row)

18. Europe Falls Once More into the Breach (headline for a story on European disunity)

19. The Kindest Cut of All (headline for an article about laser surgery)

20. All the World's Their Stage (headline for an article about terrorists)

ANSWERS

1. Commenting on the death of the Thane of Cawdor, Malcolm says, "Nothing in his life became him like the leaving it." (*Macbeth,* I, 4, 7) 2. Polonius advises his son, Laertes, "Neither a borrower nor a lender be." (*Hamlet,* I, 3, 75) 3. Romeo and Juliet are described as "a pair of star-cross'd lovers." (*Romeo and Juliet,* Prologue 6) 4. King Lear laments that he is "a man more sinn'd against than sinning." (*King Lear,* III, 2, 60) 5. In his famous soliloquy, Hamlet asks, "Whether 'tis nobler in the mind to suffer/The slings and arrows of outrageous fortune,/Or to take arms against a sea of troubles." (*Hamlet,* III, 1, 56–58)

6. A punning reference to the famous sleepwalking scene in Macbeth. Lady Macbeth imagines blood on her hands and exclaims, "Out, damn'd spot." (*Macbeth,* V, 1, 35) 7. Antony says in his funeral oration, "I come to bury Caesar, not to praise him." (*Julius Caesar,* III, 2, 74) 8. The ghost of the murdered Banquo appears at the Macbeths' banquet and ruins what might otherwise have been the social event of the year. (*Macbeth,* III, 4) 9. Casca reports on the offering of the crown to Caesar: "And still as he refus'd it, the rabblement howted and clapp'd their chopp'd hands and threw up their sweaty night-caps." (*Julius Caesar,* I, 2, 243) 10. Polonius comments on Hamlet's strange behavior: "Though this be madness, yet there is method in't." (*Hamlet,* II, 2, 205)

11. Macbeth laments the loss of "sleep that knits up the ravel'd sleave of care." (*Macbeth,* II, 2, 34) 12. Iago pretends that he is just a naive man who "will wear my heart upon my sleeve." (*Othello,* I, 1, 64) 13. Sir Toby says to Malvolio, "Dost thou think because thou art virtuous there shall be no more cakes and ale?" (*Twelfth Night,* II, 3, 114) 14. Viewing the play within a play, Queen Gertrude observes, "The lady doth protest too much, methinks." (*Hamlet,* III, 2, 230) 15. *Richard III* opens with the lines "Now is the winter of our discontent/Made glorious summer by this son of York."

16. Cleopatra sighs for her "salad days,/When I was green in judgment, cold in blood." (*Antony and Cleopatra,* I, 5, 73–74) 17. Disguised as a judge, Portia proclaims that "The quality of mercy is not strain'd,/It droppeth as the gentle rain from heaven." (*The Merchant of Venice,* IV, 1, 184–185) 18. Henry V exhorts his troops at Harfleur, "Once more unto the breach, dear friends, once more; or close the wall up with our English dead." (*Henry V,* III, 1, 1–2) 19. In his funeral oration, Antony points to Caesar's body and cries, "This was the most unkindest cut of all." (*Julius Caesar,* III, 2, 183) 20. Jaques talks about life in a dramatic fashion: "All the world's a stage,/And all the men and women merely players." (*As You Like It,* II, 7)

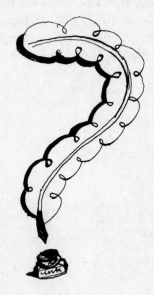

INDEX

■